Extraordinary Living
365 days of inspiration

AJI R. MICHAEL

REDEFINING LIVING

EXTRAORDINARY LIVING
365 days of inspiration

Copyright Aji R. Michael, 2023.

Book design: Aji R. Michael

Published by Redefining Living (redefiningliving.org)

Redefining Living books may be purchased for educational, business, or sales promotional use. For information, please e-mail hello@redefiningliving.org

ISBN: 978-1-8383923-4-5 (paperback)
ISBN: 978-1-8383923-5-2 (hardback)

All rights reserved.

Except for brief quotes and scriptures, no portion of this book may be reproduced, distributed, or transmitted in any form or by any means without the prior written permission of the author. Any internet addresses (websites, quotes, blogs, etc.) in this book are offered as a resource. They are not intended in any way to be or imply an endorsement by Redefining Living, nor does Redefining Living vouch for the content of these sites for the life of this book.

INTRODUCTION

Dear Reader,

Welcome to a sanctuary of grace and inspiration. This book is your three-hundred-and sixty-five-page guide to a new way of thinking about your daily routine. It is the path that transcends the ordinary, inviting you to embark on a year-long voyage of a more empowered you, faithfulness, and rejuvenation.

Giving you a back story before your pilgrimage through the "Extraordinary Living" pages is decent.

A Journey Unveiled

At the first conception, Extraordinary Living was not meant to be a book. After losing my job, no; after being forced to leave my director-level role, writing a book was the least on my mind. When I want to describe how I felt, the word I reached for the most was discombobulated. Maybe I am exaggerating with discombobulation, but it is not so easy to articulate how I felt after spending months in a toxic and traumatised work environment. It carries its own dark middle-of-the-night fear. I resent it all. I want to be left, quietly, alone. My ego wants to fight - take them to the tribunal, get revenge, and make some money. I took the case to my judicial council (inner circle), and it was decided to let it go for various reasons. One, the fact that you can win a fight doesn't mean you should get into the ring. Two, to make a headline, choose a befitting opponent.

Third, trusting God is always classy; only the divine knows what's best. So, I didn't need to conduct an autopsy on why or how the job didn't work out.

Extraordinary Living came so easily to me as a child, where the world was a playground of endless possibilities. But I wrongly thought it was shameful, so I put it away in the rush towards adulthood. It had nothing to do with our lofty goals - not in any grand objective sense. When I was young, it came from a deep engagement with my community – friends and family, the quality of experience accompanying those shared moments. I worked hard to suppress all those things. I thought it was what I had to do to grow up. It took years of work, years of careful forgetting. I never realised what I was losing.

Navigating the Depths of Vulnerability

In the course of my own existence, there have been many chapters of life detours. From the dazzling heights of career success to the unforeseen detour marked by divorce, loss of material wealth, debt, and health challenges, to name a few. But this particular time is different. I found myself standing at the crossroads of vulnerability. In the echoes of that low state, where the dark night seemed to stretch infinitely, I discovered an unexpected sanctuary—writing. Little did I know, this was the sacred ground where the seeds of "Extraordinary Living" were sown.

I first registered Extraordinary Living as a business, but the whispers won't stop. On one of my usual walks, flirting with life, it became apparent that Extraordinary Living wants to be birthed through me. The words emerged as my solace and guide from this cocoon of vulnerability. It was amidst this creative introspection that I found the extraordinary within the ordinary. As I began crafting these passages, I unearthed a profound truth: extraordinary is not always found in grand gestures but often in the delicate dance of the little things, a path woven through the ordinary moments of our lives. Each entry is an invitation to rediscover the beauty tucked within the simplicity of existence.

Discovering Grace in the Ordinary

Life has an exquisite way of revealing its magic every day—a warm cup of tea on a rainy afternoon, watering my plants in and around the house, embracing my friends in times of need, and the laughter that echoes through our shared moments. It was amidst these simple scenes that I discovered the alchemy of grace, transforming the ordinary into the extraordinary.

In the quiet moments of writing, I found solace and inspiration. It was as if grace itself danced on the tip of my keyboard, turning words into whispers of encouragement and beams of light. The journey from that low state to the creation of this jewel has been a pilgrimage of the heart that celebrates the profound grace hidden in the seemingly mundane.

As you turn the pages, let each reflection remind you that even in the smallest moments, there resides the extraordinary.

Inviting Style into the Sacred Space

The first place to start experiencing Extraordinary Living is not in the world around you but in yourself. Your mind. You're going to see yourself as a constituent of this universe, an offspring of God, and you have a right to savour the beauty of each day. If you don't believe in any form of deity outside yourself, that's okay. I can resonate with that experience as it stems from our stories about God. On this extraordinary journey, I invite you to choose your delusion. Instead, wouldn't you tell a good story that feels better and drives you forward rather than a story that disempowers and holds you back? They're both stories. They're both delusions.

Which one serves you more?

In crafting these passages, I sought to convey thoughts and curate an experience—a journey of style and grace. Each word is a brushstroke on the canvas of your day, inviting you to contemplate, resonate, and immerse yourself in the subtleties of the present.

As you embark on this extraordinary journey, consider this book a daily retreat— a sanctuary where you are free to explore the depths of your soul, draw strength from faith, and revel in the beauty of life's minutiae.

Embracing Extraordinary Living

This book has 365 entries—a complete revolution around the sun, where each day unfolds as a precious gift of reflection, inspiration, and prayer. The theme is a pilgrimage through the dual realms of time—a journey that embraces both the rhythmic routine of Chronos and the divine moments of Kairos. On each page, the divine reveals itself in countless forms, inviting you to live each day with reverence, purpose, and an awareness of the extraordinary in every temporal and timeless note.

While the entries span a year, their essence lies in adaptability. Extraordinary life is not bound by the calendar but is shaped by the melody of your own journey. Let each page become a canvas for your unique rhythm, an opportunity to infuse your days with inspiration, style, and grace.

Each daily entry consists of three sections:

Elevate Your Reflections

Immerse yourself in daily passages crafted with elegance and style, encouraging moments of profound reflection. These words are a compass guiding you through the tapestry of your soul, urging you to uncover the extraordinary within the ordinary.

Inspiration Woven with Intricacy

Let the words on these pages be your muse, guiding you with style and sophistication towards a life of purpose and meaning. The inspirational messages are crafted to resonate with the melody of your heart, urging you to dance to the rhythm of your extraordinary journey.

Prayers Adorned with Grace:

Engage in heartfelt prayers that echo the desires of your soul. Infused with grace, these prayers are a conversation with the divine, a source of strength, and a catalyst for cultivating a life rooted in faith, gratitude, and divine guidance.

"Extraordinary Living" is an invitation to shift our perspective and recalibrate our senses to the subtle whispers of grace surrounding us. It is a guide to finding significance in the every day, discovering the beauty in the ordinary, and understanding that the little things are not so little after all.

Through these daily reflections, inspirational messages, and prayers, may you, too, uncover the extraordinary in the seemingly mundane. Join me on this journey, not as an escape from life's challenges but as an immersion into the depths of its beauty. Together, let us cultivate a spirit of grace, resilience, and gratitude that will transform each day into a masterpiece of extraordinary living.

Extraordinary Living
365 days of inspiration

BALANCE

DAY 1

THE GRAND UNVEILING

Reflection

The New Year unfolds like a curtain on a grand stage. In the tapestry of life, change is the vibrant thread that weaves extraordinary stories. What change lies behind the scenes of your imagined life? Today, embrace the gift of a blank canvas of the New Year for the opportunities for growth and transformation.

Inspiration

Change is the only constant in life. Embrace, learn from, and let it mould you into the person you are meant to be. Today, let the world witness the grand unveiling of your unique story. Remember, life is an art, and change is the palette that allows us to paint extraordinary masterpieces.

Prayer

Creator of Beauty, may the stage of my life be adorned with grace. Fashion my days, O Creator, into a work of art. As the curtain rises on this New Year, guide me in the dance of change, adding bold strokes and subtle nuances revealing the beauty of my extraordinary living. Amen.

DAY 2

SETTING INTENTIONS

Reflection

Intention is the compass that guides your journey. What positive changes do you want to bring into your life? What intentions will you set for the path of extraordinary living?

Inspiration

Setting intentions is like selecting the fabrics for a couture gown. Choose with care, for each choice shapes the design of your destiny.

Prayer

Designer of Destinies, help me carefully choose the intentions that will craft the masterpiece of my extraordinary living. May my daily goals align with Your grand design.
Amen.

DAY 3

ELEGANCE IN TRANSFORMATION

Reflection

Consider the grace of a butterfly in transformation - elegant, purposeful. How can your journey of change be adorned with the same finesse that turns the ordinary into the extraordinary?

Inspiration

Like a butterfly emerging from its cocoon, your transformation can be a dance of grace and beauty. Embrace the elegance that change offers, letting the beauty of your becoming unfold with grace and poise.

Prayer

Divine Choreographer, guide my steps in the dance of transformation. Guide me as I unfold into the person I am meant to be. May the process be as elegant as the result, as I become the masterpiece you envisioned. Amen.

DAY 4

FASHIONING CHANGE WITH FLAIR

Reflection

Change is your runway; flaunt it with flair and grab the opportunity to fashion your life with grace and style. How can you infuse a sense of style into every change you encounter?

Inspiration

Like a skilled designer creating a masterpiece, craft your life with intention. Each stitch of change adds a touch of elegance to your extraordinary living.

Prayer

Divine Designer, guide my hands as I tailor my life. Grant me the confidence to fashion my life with flair. May every change be a stroke of artistic genius, reflecting the elegance of Your design. Amen.

DAY 5

RADIANCE IN REINVENTION

Reflection

Reinvention is a shimmering process, like a diamond revealing new facets. Consider your vision for this season; how can you illuminate your life through the art of reinvention?

Inspiration

Reinvention is not a reset; it's a polishing of the soul. As a diamond is shaped by gentle polishing, let the new year refine your radiance. Every facet of change adds brilliance to your extraordinary living.

Prayer

Sculptor of Souls, carve away the unnecessary, revealing the sparkle within. May each change be a step toward a more luminous version of myself. Amen.

DAY 6

CULTIVATING A SIGNATURE STYLE OF CHANGE

Reflection

Just as a signature style sets you apart, how can you cultivate a unique approach to change that reflects your essence? Think about your change anchors; what are they?

Inspiration

Change with flair, and let it be a signature style that whispers, 'This is how I navigate the extraordinary journey of life.'

Prayer

Stylish Guide, help me curate a signature style of change. May my journey be a testament to the unique and elegant individuality you've given me. Amen.

DAY 7

THE HAUTE COUTURE OF RESILIENCE

Reflection

Resilience is the fabric that withstands the tests of time. How can you dress yourself in the haute couture of resilience? When you do, wear it with pride.

Inspiration

Resilience, like haute couture, is crafted with precision. Adorn yourself with threads of strength and wear each challenge as a badge of honour.

Prayer

Artisan of Resilience, clothe me in the finest threads of strength. As I face challenges, may I wear the haute couture of resilience with grace and unwavering confidence. Amen.

DAY 8

THE RUNWAY OF RESILIENCE

Reflection

Resilience is not just enduring; it's walking the runway of challenges with grace. How can you showcase resilience as a chic and powerful quality?

Inspiration

Resilience is the most stylish response to adversity. Strut down the runway of challenges with poise, for every stumble is a chance to showcase the strength that defines your extraordinary living.

Prayer

Empowerer of Hearts, may I walk with grace and resilience. Clothe me in the fabric of strength as I navigate change challenges. May I walk the runway of challenges gracefully, showcasing the power within. Amen.

DAY 9

THE ELEGANCE OF LETTING GO

Reflection

Letting go is a dance of elegance. What can you release to create space for the extraordinary in your life? Release what no longer serves you.

Inspiration

Release is not loss; it's the art of creating space for new blessings. Dance with elegance as you let go, trusting in the beauty of the unknown.

Prayer

Gentle Guide, help me shed the layers that weigh me down. May I release with grace, knowing each goodbye is a hello to a more extraordinary life. May the elegance of letting go bring freedom to my extraordinary living. Amen.

DAY 10

REDEFINING THE NORM

Reflection

Extraordinary living often starts with the courage to redefine the boundaries of standards. Consider challenging the status quo that binds you and redefining your norm.

Inspiration

Norms are but threads woven by society. Break free, brush strokes of courage redefine the ordinary, creating a masterpiece of your unique expression.

Prayer

Dear Creator, grant me the courage to redefine norms limiting my potential. Help me create a life that reflects the uniqueness with which you've designed me. Amen.

DAY 11

A WALK ON THE RUNWAY OF POSSIBILITIES

Reflection

Imagine your life as a runway, each step a possibility waiting to be embraced. How can you walk boldly into the endless possibilities of the New Year?

Inspiration

Every step holds the promise of a new possibility. Walk boldly, knowing that the runway of life is yours to conquer.

Prayer

Guide of Possibilities: may I walk the runway of life with confidence and purpose. Lead me to embrace the extraordinary possibilities that lie ahead. Guide my steps on the runway of possibilities, and may I walk with confidence, embracing the opportunities that unfold with each stride. Amen.

DAY 12

ACCESSORISING WITH GRATITUDE

Reflection

Gratitude is the timeless accessory that complements every outfit of life. Think about the past days; what are you grateful for? How can you adorn your days with the elegance of gratitude?

Inspiration

Like a classic piece of jewellery, gratitude never goes out of style. Adorn your moments with its sparkle and watch how it enhances the beauty of your extraordinary living.

Prayer

Graceful Giver, teach me to accessorise my days with a thankful heart. May gratitude be the stylish accessory that defines my extraordinary being. Amen.

DAY 13

THE TIMELESS APPEAL OF LETTING GO

Reflection

Letting go is not just a cliche; it's a timeless practice that allows for new beginnings. What can you release toDay to make space for the extraordinary?

Inspiration

The art of letting go is a timeless classic, like a chic wardrobe essential. Release with style and invite the fresh breeze of new possibilities into your life.

Prayer

Custodian of Timeless Beauty, grant me the strength to let go gracefully. May my releases be as graceful as the changing seasons, allowing for a collection of new experiences. I affirm each release is a step towards a more beautiful and extraordinary life. Amen.

DAY 14

CONFIDENCE IN CHANGE: STRUTTING YOUR STUFF

Reflection

Change is your personal runway, and confidence is the stiletto that elevates your walk through life's changes. How can you exude confidence and style as you navigate the catwalk of life's transformations?

Inspiration

"Change is your runway, and confidence is your stiletto. Strut through it with the confidence of a fashion icon, knowing that every step is a declaration of your extraordinary self.

Prayer

Provider of Confidence, lace up my spirit with the confidence to strut boldly through the seasons of life. May I stride through life with elegance and poise. Amen.

DAY 15

DRESSING YOUR DAYS IN PURPOSE

Reflection

Every Day is a canvas waiting for purposeful strokes. Like a well-curated wardrobe, how can you carefully select your actions, turning them into a masterpiece of extraordinary living?

Inspiration

Your intention is the fabric that weaves purpose into your day. Dress each moment with the elegance of purpose, creating a closet of meaningful experiences.

Prayer

Designer of Destiny, guide me as I dress my days in purpose. May every choice be intentional, creating a stylish tapestry of an extraordinary life. Amen.

DAY 16

GLAMOUR IN ADVERSITY

Reflection

Adversity is not a fashion faux pas; it's an opportunity to showcase your resilience with glamour. How can you turn challenges into moments of extraordinary beauty?

Inspiration

Glamour is not reserved for the perfect; it shines bright even in adversity. Adorn your challenges with the sparkle of resilience.

Prayer

Artisan of Resilience, may I find the sparkle within, even amid challenges. May every challenge I face be an opportunity to shine with the radiance of my extraordinary spirit. Amen.

DAY 17

THE RADIANCE OF LIVING IN THE PRESENT

Reflection

Radiance is born in the present moment. It is in the present moment that a miracle happens.

In your day, think of artistic ways you can illuminate your life with the vibrant colours of the now.

Inspiration

Radiance is born in the present. Let go of the shadows of the past and the uncertainties of the future, bask in the luminosity of the present moment and let your life shine.

Prayer

Divine Illuminator, guide me to live in the brilliance of the present. May I be mindful of the beauty surrounding me and let it reflect in my extraordinary living.

DAY 18

GENTLE NUDGES OF CHANGE: WHISPERS OF COUTURE WISDOM

Reflection

Change whispers gently, offering couture wisdom for your journey, nudging you towards growth. How can you attune your ears to the subtle guidance of transformation?

Inspiration

Couture wisdom whispers in the stillness of change, guiding you toward refinement. Listen closely, for it holds the secrets to an extraordinary life.

Prayer

Wisdom Weaver, open my ears to the subtle nudges of change. May the whispers guide me toward the elegance of extraordinary living. Amen.

DAY 19

SCULPTING SELF-LOVE

Reflection

Self-love is the sculptor of your inner masterpiece. Every curve and contour tell a story of self-acceptance. Spend some time toDay to nurture your contour and scars, both past and present.

Inspirational

Self-love is the most elegant sculpture you can create. Let each act of self-care be a stroke, moulding a work of art that radiates with the beauty of your extraordinary self.

Prayer

Lover of my Soul, mould my heart with the clay of self-love. May I appreciate the beauty of my life detour and use it to sculpt a life filled with love. May the masterpiece of my self-appreciation be a testament to the extraordinary love you've poured into me. Amen.

DAY 20

CULTIVATING A CLOSET OF HEALTHY HABITS

Reflection

Just as a well-curated wardrobe enhances your style, healthy habits are the stylish ensembles that outfit your life. Take some time out this week to curate a collection of habits that elevate your well-being.

Inspiration

Health is the most fashionable accessory, and healthy habits are the timeless classics of your life closet. Choose them wisely and watch your overall well-being flourish.

Prayer

Life Giver, guide me in cultivating a wardrobe of healthy habits. May each choice affirm my commitment to an extraordinary and vibrant life. Amen.

DAY 21

TIMELESS FASHION: CONQUERING THE UNKNOWN

Reflection

Fearless fashion is the fragrance of a trendsetter, embracing the unknown with style. When was the last time you boldly step into uncharted territory? Consider your vision for this season; how can you turn them into opportunities for bold living?

Inspiration

Uncertainty is your runway; walk it with confidence. Every step into the unknown is a chance to showcase your courage and let the runway of life be yours to savour.

Prayer

Courageous God, wrap me in the cloak of courage. Grace my path with divine light, and may I stride through the unknown with the boldness of a fashion icon. May my uncertainties transform into opportunities for extraordinary growth. Amen.

DAY 22

SAUNTERING THROUGH NEW OPPORTUNITIES

Reflection

Opportunities are invitations to a stylish dance. Let this year be your year of yes. Waltz gracefully through the ballroom and let the rhythm of possibility guide your steps. Are there opportunities lurking around you? Say yes; it's a win: win, after all.

Inspiration

Life's dance floor is crowded with a buffet of opportunities. Gracefully waltz through, knowing that every step adds a touch of elegance to your extraordinary journey.

Prayer

Choreographer of Life, teach me the dance of grace. May I saunter through new opportunities with poise, and may each opportunity be a chance to showcase the beauty of my extraordinary self. Amen.

DAY 23

SPARKLE IN THE SMALL WINS

Reflection

The sparkle of success is not confined to grand achievements; small wins are the shimmering details that add sparkle to your journey. Find brilliance in the small wins that spiced your journey. How can you celebrate the little triumphs today?

Inspiration

Like a finely embellished garment, small wins add sparkle and elevate the overall elegance of your extraordinary living.

Prayer

Master of Celebration, adorn me with the grace to appreciate the brilliance in the small victories. May each triumph be a dazzling moment filled with joy and make my journey extraordinary. Amen.

DAY 24

CULTIVATING A CLOSET OF JOY

Reflection

Joy is not just an emotion; it's a wardrobe choice. Imagine your joy as a wardrobe, with each emotion representing a different ensemble. How can you cultivate a closet filled with joy today?

Inspiration

Joy is the most stylish accessory you can wear. Cultivate a closet filled with its colours, choosing the hues that resonate with the melody of your extraordinary life.

Prayer

Source of Joy, help me in curating a closet of joy. May I choose joy as my daily attire and spread its contagious beauty to those around me. May every emotion I wear reflect an extraordinary existence's vibrant and harmonious tones. Amen.

DAY 25

RITUALS OF CHANGE: A SERENE MORNING ROUTINE

Reflection

Your morning rituals are not just routines; they are ceremonies that set the tone for your day. Do you have a rhythm for your mornings? If not, consider how to infuse your essence into your morning rituals for a Day of extraordinary living.

Inspiration

Your morning routine is the rehearsal for the day's performance. Let each ritual be a statement of intent for an extraordinary day.

Prayer

Possessor of Day and night, infuse my morning rituals with your fragrance. May my every step be a dance of purpose and every ritual a proclamation of my commitment to an extraordinary life. Amen.

DAY 26

ADORNING YOUR SPACE WITH POSITIVITY

Reflection

The ambience of your space affects your spirit. Decorate your room with positivity and let it reflect your inner elegance. How can you positively adorn your surroundings, creating an environment that nurtures your soul?

Inspiration

Positivity is the interior design of your life. Adorn it with elements that bring joy, peace, and inspiration into your extraordinary sanctuary.

Prayer

Dear God, inspire me to adorn my space with positivity. May my surroundings reflect the elegance and tranquillity of an extraordinary haven. Amen.

DAY 27

TRUSTING GOD'S TIMING EFFORTLESSLY

Reflection

Trusting divine timing is like wearing an effortlessly chic garment. Though your faith is tested, exercise your patience, but you'll instead be a dreamer than a settler. How can you surrender to the rhythm of God's plan, embracing the timeless allure of patience?

Inspiration

Trust in the divine rhythm, and let your life unfold with the grace of a timeless fashion statement, knowing that every moment is a carefully curated piece of your extraordinary journey.

Prayer

Divine Presence, help me not to focus so much on what I don't have that I miss out on all your blessings. Instil in me the patience to trust your timing, and may I navigate life with the effortless chic that comes from surrendering to your divine plan. Amen.

DAY 28

THE STATEMENT PIECE OF FORGIVENESS

Reflection

Forgiveness is not just an action; it's the statement piece that transforms your heart and completes the healing ensemble. Are there people and events that you need to forgive? What would it look like if you adorn yourself with the bold and powerful accessory of forgiveness today?

Inspiration

Forgiveness is like Eau de parfum; wear it boldly, for its transformative power adds fragrance to your extraordinary life.

Prayer

Artisan of Healing, teach me the art of forgiveness. May my heart be adorned with the bold and transformative beauty of letting go. May forgiveness be the bold accessory that completes my extraordinary living.
Amen.

DAY 29

THE TIMELESS HABIT OF COMMITMENT TO GROWTH

Reflection

Commitment to growth is the timeless habit that shapes your journey. Consider your envisioned life; how can you cultivate a commitment to continual growth, ensuring that each Day is a step that leads you to an extraordinary life?

Inspiration

Commitment to growth is an eternal style that never fades. Wear it like a classic piece of jewellery daily, allowing it to be the focal point of your extraordinary existence.

Prayer

Everlasting God, help me cultivate the timeless habit of commitment to growth. May my dedication to continual improvement become contagious to others. Amen.

DAY 30

COUTURE OF CONNECTION: NURTURING RELATIONSHIPS

Reflection

Nurturing relationships is not just a social skill; it's the couture that weaves the fabric of a fulfilling life. Who's in your circle, or who's circle are you in? If you're unsure, think about how you can weave a couture of connection, ensuring the threads of your relationships are strong, vibrant, and filled with love.

Inspiration

Each relationship is a piece of couture, unique and crafted with care. Nurturing connections with love, understanding, and authenticity transforms the fabric of our lives into a masterpiece of extraordinary living.

Prayer

Dear Counsellor, guide me in nurturing the connections that enrich my life. May every interaction be a stitch that strengthens my life's bonds of love and compassion. Amen.

DAY 31

THE GLITTER OF GRATITUDE

Reflection

Gratitude is not just an attitude; it's the glitter that enhances the beauty of your journey.

Are you used to being your own worst critic? If so, it may feel uncomfortable to shift your focus and see yourself through the lens of gratitude. As you pause and express appreciation for everything in your life, take time to thank and celebrate yourself unapologetically.

Inspiration

Being truly grateful for yourself, not just when you get it right but also when you mess up, is what living with confidence, boldness, and beauty looks like.

Prayer

Dear Source, teach me the art of gratitude. May I express thanks sincerely, befitting the extraordinary gifts life bestows upon me. Amen.

DAY 32

THE GENTLE STRENGTH OF LOVE

Reflection

Take a moment to reflect on moments when love has been a source of your strength and inspiration. Reflect on the gentle yet unyielding strength that love acquires when rooted in humility. How did it make you feel?

Inspiration

The mightiest strength is found in the gentlest acts of love. Today, embrace the foundational power of love. Let it guide your thoughts, words, and actions.

Prayer

Divine Creator, thank you for the gift of love that surrounds and fills my life. May my actions be a testament to the extraordinary impact of love expressed with a humble heart. And may I be a vessel of love, reflecting your grace in all I do. Amen.

DAY 33

FINDING EXTRAORDINARY STRENGTH

Reflection

Consider a time when embracing humility allows you to find extraordinary strength amid life's challenges. How did it make you feel?

Inspiration

In the crucible of adversity, humility becomes the alchemist that transforms challenges into extraordinary strength. Today, face life's detours with the resilience that arises from a humble heart.

Prayer

Divine Comforter, grant me the humility
to face life's challenges gracefully.
May my challenges become stepping stones
to extraordinary strength, and may humility
be my anchor. Amen.

DAY 34

UNVEILING INNER WISDOM HUMILITY'S LUMINOUS EFFECT

Reflection

Take some time to delve into the profound meaning of humility. Reflect on how embracing humility unveils inner wisdom, making it a bright beacon.

Inspirational

When embraced with humility, love becomes a radiant force that lights up the darkest corners of our existence. Today, let the luminosity of love shine forth, guided by the humility within.

Prayer

Divine Source of Wisdom, guide me to the depth of humility. May humility be the flame that brightens my path, creating extraordinary brilliance in my actions and relationships. Amen.

DAY 35

LOVE'S TRANSFORMATIVE POWER: HUMILITY AS CATALYST

Reflection

Ponder the transformative power of love with humility as the graceful partner. Reflect on how humility can unlock the extraordinary potential for positive change and growth.

Inspiration

Virtue is a dance, and humility is its graceful partner. Today, let the dance of kindness, patience, and humility guide your steps, creating an extraordinary ballet of character.

Prayer

Custodian of Humility, infuse my heart with the transformative power of love. May humility be the spark that turns ordinary moments into extraordinary opportunities for growth and connection. Amen.

DAY 36

HUMILITY IN SERVICE: LOVE EXPRESSED THROUGH ACTIONS

Reflection

Reflect on the intense connection between humility and service. Consider how expressing Love through humble actions not only transforms the lives of others but also elevates your own existence.

Inspiration

Love that expects nothing in return is the purest form of Love. Today, let your Love be a gift freely given, with no strings attached.

Prayer

Divine Love, help me love without reason, mirroring your boundless and unconditional Love. May my actions reflect the Love you have poured into my life, creating ripples of kindness that touch the extraordinary in others. Amen.

DAY 37

LOVE'S SUBTLE SYMPHONY

Reflection

If Love were a song, consider the symphony playing in the background of your life and reflect on the harmony that comes when this is the guiding melody in your interactions.

Inspiration

Love and humility dance together in a subtle symphony. Today, let your heart play the notes of compassion and allow humility to be the conductor, guiding you to an extraordinary crescendo of kindness.

Prayer

Divine Love, tune my heart to the frequency of Love. May my life be a symphony that echoes your divine melody, filling the world with the extraordinary sound of Love. Amen.

DAY 38

LOVE'S RIPPLE EFFECT: CULTIVATING COMPASSION

Reflection

Reflect on how your small loving gestures can create waves of extraordinary kindness. Think about ways you can cultivate compassion in your daily interactions.

Inspirational

Compassion is the language the heart speaks. In a world that sometimes seems cold, choose to warm it with the fires of empathy. Today, let your compassion shine brightly.

Prayer

God of compassion, teach me to see others with the eyes of Love. May my actions reflect the kindness you have shown me. May my gestures inspire an extraordinary wave of compassion in the world. Amen.

DAY 39

JOY IN THE JOURNEY

Reflection

Take a moment to appreciate the journey of life. Reflect on the joy that can be found in the present moment, regardless of circumstances.

Inspiration

Joy is not found in the destination but in the journey. Today, savour the moments of laughter, embrace the challenges with a hopeful spirit, and find joy in the ordinary.

Prayer

Heavenly Father, thank you for the gift of life's journey. May I find joy in every step, knowing that you walk with me through every joy and challenge. Amen.

DAY 40

APPRECIATING SIMPLE BEGINNINGS

Reflection

As you embark on this extraordinary journey, reflect on the profound simplicity of small steps. Visualise your potential for growth and beauty that lies in the modest roots of your aspirations.

Inspiration

In the garden of life, humble beginnings are the seeds of extraordinary growth. Today, embrace the beauty of starting small, knowing that every journey of significance begins with a single step.

Prayer

Gracious Creator, grant me the humility to appreciate the value of small beginnings. May the dawn of this Day mark the beginning of a life infused with Love. Illuminate my path with the radiance of your Love, guiding me toward virtue and extraordinary living. Amen.

DAY 41

LOVE'S COMPASS

Reflection

Love never fails isn't just a cliché; it's proven valid many times. Ponder the role of love as a compass in your journey. Reflect on how it guides your direction and directs you toward an extraordinary life.

Inspiration

Love is the compass that steers us through the vast landscapes of life. Today, let your heart be guided by the magnetic force of love, navigating toward the extraordinary.

Prayer

Guiding Light of Love, be my compass in this journey. May my steps be directed by the north of your love, leading me toward an extraordinary destination. Amen.

DAY 42

LOVE'S RESILIENCE

Reflection

Love always wins. Consider the resilience that love brings in the face of challenges. Reflect on how love transforms obstacles into stepping stones in your life or others.

Inspiration

Love is the resilient force that transforms stumbling blocks into stepping stones. Today, face every situation with the unwavering power of love, turning obstacles into extraordinary experiences.

Prayer

Eternal Source of Love, infuse me with the strength of love. May challenges be opportunities for extraordinary growth, and love be the guiding force in my every step.
Amen.

DAY 43

LOVE'S REFLECTION

Reflection

Take a moment to gaze into the mirror of your actions. Reflect on the attribute that shapes the reflection staring back at you; they add depth and authenticity to your journey or subtract from it.

Inspiration

The mirror reflects not just an image but the depth of love within. Today, desire the reflection of a humble heart and let it be the extraordinary signature on the canvas of your life.

Prayer

Spirit of Truth, reveal the depths of love within me. May my reflection be a testament to the extraordinary beauty of embracing humility in every step. Amen.

DAY 44

GRATITUDE AS AN EXPRESSION OF LOVE

Reflection

Reflect on the blessings in your life, both big and small. Consider how expressing gratitude can deepen your connection with others. Express gratitude to three people today.

Inspiration

Gratitude is the melody of the heart. Today, play the symphony of thankfulness. Notice the beauty in the ordinary, and let gratitude be your song.

Prayer

Gracious God, thank you for the abundance of blessings in my life. May my heart overflow with gratitude, and may I share that gratitude with those around me. Amen.

DAY 45

THE ART OF LISTENING

Reflection

Take a moment to reflect on the art of listening. Consider how humility opens the door to genuinely hearing others, fostering connection, intimacy and understanding.

Inspiration

In the silence of humility, the art of listening flourishes. Today, be present in your conversations and let the extraordinary unfold as you humbly listen, embracing the wisdom of others.

Prayer

Divine Listener, attune my heart to the voices around me, both spoken and unspoken. May humility be the instrument that allows me to hear the extraordinary stories and lessons woven into the fabric of humanity. Amen.

DAY 46

THE ART OF FORGIVENESS

Reflection

Consider the weight that comes with holding onto grudges. Reflect on the freedom that forgiveness brings to your spirit.

Inspiration

Forgiveness is the key that unlocks the chains of resentment. Today, choose the path of freedom. Forgive others as you have been forgiven.

Prayer

Merciful God, grant me the strength to forgive as you have forgiven me. Release me from the burden of resentment and fill my heart with your Love. Amen.

DAY 47

VIRTUOUS LIVING: THE ELEGANCE OF HUMBLE CHOICES

Reflection

Ponder the peace that accompanies humble choices in daily living. Reflect on how each decision made with humility adds a touch of grace to the tapestry of your life.

Inspiration

Elegance is found in the humble choices we make. Today, embrace the stylish grace that comes with virtuous living, allowing humility to be the Designer of your extraordinary choices.

Prayer

Divine Designer, clothe me in the elegance of humble choices. May my decisions reflect the virtues within, creating an extraordinary tapestry of a virtuous life. Amen.

DAY 48

THE ART OF HUMBLE LEADERSHIP: LEADING WITH LOVE

Reflection

Consider the artistry of humble leadership; what does it mean to you? Reflect on how leading with Love and humility transforms ordinary roles into extraordinary opportunities to inspire and uplift others.

Inspiration

The art of leadership is painted with strokes of Love and humility. Today, step into the role of a humble leader, creating a masterpiece of inspiration that resonates in the hearts of those you lead.

Prayer

Heavenly Artist, guide my hand as I paint the canvas of leadership. May love and humility be the colours that bring vibrancy and depth to the art of leading. Amen.

DAY 49

LOVE'S REFLECTION: MIRRORING EXTRAORDINARY RELATIONSHIPS

Reflection

Take a moment to gaze into the mirror of your relationships. Reflect on the attribute that shapes the reflection staring back at you; they add depth and authenticity to your connections or subtract from it.

Inspiration

Love is the mirror that reflects the extraordinary in our relationships. Today, desire the reflection of Love within your connections and let it be the remarkable signature on the canvas of your life.

Prayer

Divine Love, reveal the depths of Love within my relationships. May my interactions be a testament to the extraordinary beauty that comes from embracing Love in every connection. Amen.

DAY 50

THE MINIMALIST APPEAL OF PATIENCE

Reflection

Patience is not just a virtue; it's the cornerstone of a minimalist and gracious life. Consider the role of patience in your life and reflect on how patience is woven together, allowing for growth and transformation.

Inspiration

Minimalism in patience brings elegance to your character. Simplify your life by allowing each moment to unfold at its own pace. Today, embrace the unfolding of time, trusting each moment is a stepping stone toward a greater purpose.

Prayer

God of patience, teach me to trust in your perfect timing. Grant me the patience to endure and the wisdom to see the beauty in waiting. May my patience bring a sense of calm and elegance to my extraordinary living. Amen.

DAY 51

CULTIVATING A PERFUME OF MINDFULNESS

Reflection

Mindfulness is not just a practice; the subtle perfume transforms the atmosphere around you, making every moment exquisite. How can you cultivate a perfume of mindfulness, filling your days with the sweet scent of Presence?

Inspiration

Let mindfulness be the perfume you wear. Cultivate its fragrance, and let it infuse every moment with the essence of extraordinary living.

Prayer

Divine Presence, help me cultivate the perfume of mindfulness. May my awareness linger in the air, creating an atmosphere of grace and transforming each moment into a luxurious experience of extraordinary living. Amen.

DAY 52

EMBRACING SACRED SILENCE

Reflection

Amid life's symphony, there is a powerful pause. How often do you embrace the sacred silence with the potential for profound connection and introspection?

Inspiration

Sacred silence is the blank canvas upon which the universe paints its most intricate masterpieces. In the stillness, we find the whispers of our souls and the gentle heartbeat of the divine.

Prayer

Divine Peace, teach me the art of embracing sacred silence. May my quiet moments be adorned with the richness of your Presence, unveiling the extraordinary within the hush.
Amen.

DAY 53

A BLANK PAGE OF POSSIBILITIES

Reflection

Sacred silence is like a blank page, awaiting the words of your heart and the brushstrokes of your spirit. Think of ways to maximise the stillness as a canvas of endless possibilities?

Inspiration

Within sacred silence, every pause is a promise - a blank page inviting the ink of your dreams and the colours of your aspirations. In this quietude, you hold the brush to paint a masterpiece.

Prayer

Creator of Silence and Sound, guide my pen and brush in the sacred silence. May my expressions on this blank page be a work of art that reflects the extraordinary within and without. Amen.

DAY 54

NAVIGATING THE SILENCE WITHIN

Reflection

As you journey into sacred silence, what echoes and whispers do you hear within the chambers of your soul? How can you navigate the inner stillness to discover the truths in the quietude?

Inspiration

The silence within is a sacred labyrinth. Navigate its pathways with curiosity and courage, for within its hallowed halls, you'll find the keys to unlock the mysteries of your authentic self.

Prayer

Guide of Inner Silence, lead me through the labyrinth of my soul. May the echoes within reveal the hidden treasures and illuminate the path to my most extraordinary self.
Amen.

DAY 55

A SYMPHONY OF REST

Reflection

Sacred silence is a restful pause in life's symphony. Think of ways to transform the silence into a soothing symphony of rest, rejuvenating your spirit and restoring your energy?

Inspiration

Rest within the sacred silence is a melody of rejuvenation. Allow the stillness to be the gentle lullaby that cradles your spirit, bringing harmony to your mind, body, and soul.

Prayer

Lover of my Soul, orchestrate the symphony of rest within the sacred silence. May the pauses be the well-deserved interludes that replenish my energy and soothe my soul.
Amen.

DAY 56

THE HEART'S HUMBLE GLOW

Reflection

Think of a time you were with someone you'd consider humble, and reflect on how their gentle radiance illuminates your connections and conversation. How does it feel?

Inspiration

Humility is the gentle glow that radiates from the heart. Today, let your actions be bathed in this humble light, creating an extraordinary aura of kindness wherever you go.

Prayer

Heart Illuminator, kindle within me the humble glow that transforms ordinary moments into extraordinary experiences. May my heart radiate with the warmth of love and humility. Amen.

DAY 57

CONVERSATIONS BEYOND WORDS

Reflection

In sacred silence, some conversations transcend the limitations of words. How can you engage in discussions without language, where understanding flows effortlessly and the essence of connection is felt in the quiet spaces between breaths?

Inspiration

Beyond words, in sacred silence, hearts commune. Engage in these wordless dialogues, allowing your heart to speak in the language of the soul.

Prayer

Heart Whisperer, teach me the language of wordless conversations. May my moments of sacred silence be filled with the profound connections that words could never express. Amen.

DAY 58

THE SACRED SILENCE BEYOND ENDINGS

Reflection

As you transition into a new season, consider the sacred silence beyond endings. How can you embrace the stillness that follows each completion, recognising it as a gateway to new beginnings?

Inspiration

The sacred silence beyond endings is the canvas for new beginnings. In this pause, savour the lessons, honour the growth, and welcome the unknown with a heart adorned in hope and gratitude.

Prayer

Guardian of Beginnings and Endings, I find solace and anticipation in the sacred silence. May the echoes of the past guide me, and the hush of the future inspire me to live each moment in the extraordinary tapestry of life.
Amen.

DAY 59

RADIANT REFLECTIONS: CELEBRATING PROGRESS

Reflection

Take a moment to reflect on your journey. How can you celebrate your progress, acknowledging the steps you've taken towards a life of extraordinary living? Celebrate the journey as much as the destination.

Inspiration

Progress is not just a destination; it's a radiant reflection of your journey. Celebrate the small victories and the milestones, for each one, is a shimmering reflection of your extraordinary journey.

Prayer

Master of Celebrations, guide me in recognising and celebrating the progress of my journey. May each step be a blessing to myself and others. May I see the beauty in each step, and may the reflections inspire continued growth. Amen.

DAY 60

AWAKENING THE SPIRIT

Reflection

Feel the gentle stirrings of your spirit in the stillness of new beginnings. Reflect on how you embrace the potential for profound spiritual growth as you embark on this journey.

Inspiration

Just as the dawn breaks, so too can your spirit emerge from the shadows of yesterday. Today, make a commitment to awaken the dormant possibilities within.

Prayer

Divine Creator, guide me on this journey of awakening. Grant me the wisdom to recognise the power within me for new beginnings, hidden exploits and the courage to embrace spiritual growth. Amen.

DAY 61

RENEWAL OF MIND

Reflection

Today, focus on the renewing power of the mind. Using your positive affirmations, allow the transformative power to cleanse and refresh your mental landscape.

Inspiration

Your thoughts are the seeds of your destiny. In the garden of your mind, cultivate thoughts that blossom into a renewed sense of purpose and positivity.

Prayer

Eternal Source of Wisdom, renew my mind.
Help me plant the seeds of positivity and
guide my thoughts towards transformation.
Amen.

DAY 62

FAITHFUL FOUNDATIONS

Reflection

Spend some time to explore the bedrock of extraordinary living – faith. Reflect on faith as the unwavering foundation upon which you can build a life of purpose and significance.

Inspiration

Faith is the cornerstone of a life well-lived. With it, you can withstand storms and build a legacy that echoes through eternity.

Prayer

Faithful God, strengthen my foundation in faith. May my life be a testament to the unwavering belief in the extraordinary. Amen.

DAY 63

SEEDS OF CHANGE

Reflection

Today, plant the seeds of positive change. Ponder of the aspects of your life to sow the seeds that will grow into a harvest of transformation and growth.

Inspiration

Change is the heartbeat of progress. Embrace the process, for in the seeds of change, you find the roots of your future self.

Prayer

Eternal God, help me plant seeds of positivity and growth. Grant me the grace to nurture them into a bountiful harvest that transforms my life and others. Amen.

DAY 64

EMBRACING POSSIBILITIES

Reflection

Step out of your comfort zone toDay and embrace new possibilities. Extraordinary living begins when you boldly venture into the unknown.

Inspiration

Life's most incredible adventures lie beyond the familiar. Embrace the discomfort, for it is the crucible of transformation.

Prayer

Courageous Guide, grant me the courage to embrace the unknown and the faith to believe in the possibilities that await. Amen.

DAY 65

GRATITUDE JOURNALING

Reflection

In the quiet moments of reflection, recognise the power of gratitude. Practice gratitude as a tool for rejuvenation, acknowledging the blessings surrounding you.

Inspiration

Gratitude is a magnet for miracles. Let your journal be a canvas where blessings are painted and joy is found in the simple moments.

Prayer

Gracious Giver, open my eyes to the beauty around me. May gratitude be the melody that fills my heart and the fragrance of my aura. Amen.

DAY 66

MINDFUL MOMENTS

Reflection

In the busyness of your day, look for opportunities to incorporate mindful moments. Let awareness and Presence be your companions on this journey of extraordinary living.

Inspiration

Mindfulness is the key that unlocks the treasures hidden in each breath. In the present moment, discover the richness of life.

Prayer

Omnipresence God, guide me in cultivating mindfulness. May each moment be a gift and each breath a reminder of the extraordinary. Amen.

DAY 67

STEADFAST IN FAITH

Reflection

Building resilience requires unwavering belief in the unseen and the courage to stand firm in adversity. Always remember that in the crucible of challenges, the strength of your faith is tested.

Inspirational

Faith is the anchor that steadies the ship during life's storms. It's not the absence of challenges that defines us but the unwavering faith we hold onto amid them.

Prayer

Faithful Guide, grant me the resilience to face challenges with unwavering faith. May I believe in your guidance as the pillar supporting me through every trial. Amen.

DAY 68

CULTIVATING JOY

Reflection

Cultivating joy is an art that involves recognising the beauty in small moments and choosing happiness amidst life's complexities. Spend time toDay to explore the sources of joy within and around you.

Inspiration

Joy is a garden waiting to be tended. As you cultivate gratitude and embrace life's simple pleasures, you water the seeds of joy, allowing them to blossom.

Prayer

Joyful Creator, teach me to see the beauty in each day. May joy be my companion, and gratitude be the soil in which it thrives. Amen.

DAY 69

SACRED SPACES

Reflection

Create and cherish sacred spaces for personal reflection and connection. These spaces, physical or within the heart, serve as sanctuaries to commune with the divine and discover your innermost self.

Inspiration

In the quiet corners of sacred spaces, the world's noise fades, and the whispers of your soul become audible. Cherish these moments of connection.

Prayer

Sacred Presence, bless the spaces where I seek solace. May they be filled with your peace, and may my heart be open to your gentle guidance. Amen.

DAY 70

TRAILBLAZING CONFIDENCE

Reflection

Confidence is the key to unlocking the doors of an extraordinary life. Today, reflect on the strengths within you and cultivate the self-assurance needed to blaze new trails.

Inspiration

Confidence is not the absence of fear but the belief that you can thrive despite it. With each step forward, you blaze a trail of self-discovery.

Prayer

My Source of Confidence, ignite within me the courage to step boldly into the unknown. May my journey be marked by self-assurance and a fearless spirit. Amen.

DAY 71

NAVIGATING CHANGE

Reflection

Change is the only constant in life. Today, explore strategies for navigating and embracing change with a positive mindset. In change, there is the promise of growth.

Inspiration

Like a river carving its course through the landscape, change shapes the terrain of your life. Embrace it, for amid change, new landscapes of opportunity emerge.

Prayer

Divine Light, grant me the wisdom to navigate transitions with grace. May each change bring forth opportunities for growth and renewal.
Amen.

DAY 72

HEART-CENTERED LIVING

Reflection

Shift your focus towards heart-centered living and compassionate interactions. Today, reflect on recent events and how aligning your actions with your heart's kindness enhances your life's quality.

Inspiration

Bridges are built in the sanctuary of a compassionate heart, and wounds are healed. Let your actions reflect the love that resides within.

Prayer

Compassionate Source, guide my actions with the warmth of the heart. May my interactions be filled with kindness and understanding.
Amen.

DAY 73

FAITHFUL FRIENDSHIPS

Reflection

In the tapestry of life, faithful friendships are the threads that weave a story of growth, support, and shared joy. Today, reflect on the richness of those friendships that nurture your soul and contribute to your journey of becoming.

Inspiration

A faithful friend is a treasure, a constant in the ebb and flow of life. Cherish those who stand by you, offering their support and encouragement as you navigate the extraordinary path.

Prayer

Faithful Companion, bless my friendships. May I be a source of strength and encouragement, just as I receive from those who walk beside me. Amen.

DAY 74

REJUVENATION RITUALS

Reflection

Consider the rituals that rejuvenate your physical, mental, and spiritual self. Today, explore the importance of daily practices that restore and uplift every dimension of your being. If you're not being inspired, it's time for a change.

Inspiration

Rejuvenation is an art, and your daily rituals are the brushstrokes on the canvas of your life. Craft rituals that nourish your body, refresh your mind, and uplift your spirit.

Prayer

Source of Renewal, guide me in developing rituals that restore and rejuvenate. May each intentional act of self-care be a step towards extraordinary living. Amen.

DAY 75

PURPOSEFUL LIVING

Reflection

Purposeful living is the compass that directs you on your extraordinary journey. Take a moment to reflect on your personal purpose. Are your actions aligned with meaningful goals that resonate with the essence of who you are?

Inspiration

Living with purpose is like sailing with the wind at your back. Let your purpose be the guiding star, illuminating the path towards a life of significance and fulfilment.

Prayer

Guiding Light, illuminate my purpose. May my actions align with my deepest values, leading me towards a life of meaning and impact.
Amen.

DAY 76

RESILIENCE IN ADVERSITY

Reflection

Adversity is a companion on the journey of life. Reflect on a time when you've drawn strength from faith and cultivated resilience in the face of challenges. Remember, in any adversity, find the seeds of growth.

Inspiration

Resilience is the quiet strength that emerges when faced with adversity. Embrace challenges as personal and spiritual growth opportunities, knowing you are resilient beyond measure.

Prayer

Strength Giver, grant me resilience in times of adversity. I want a heart willing to be faithful to God in all seasons, not just in the seasons I planned. May my faith be a shield, and my Spirit remain unbroken in the face of life's challenges. Amen.

DAY 77

MIND-BODY CONNECTION

Reflection

Explore the profound connection between mind and body; what does this mean for you? Today, reflect on how nurturing your mind-body connection contributes to your holistic well-being and an extraordinary life.

Inspirational

The mind and body dance in harmony, each influencing the other. Cultivate mindfulness, nourish your body, and witness the symphony of well-being unfold.

Prayer

Harmony Creator, guide me in honouring the sacred connection between my mind and body. May my thoughts and actions towards myself and others contribute to my holistic well-being. Amen.

DAY 78

HARMONY IN RELATIONSHIPS

Reflection

Harmony in relationships is the sweet melody that resonates through the symphony of life. Today, think of three ways to cultivate positive energy in your connections, creating a harmonious dance of love and understanding.

Inspiration

In the garden of relationships, sow seeds of harmony. Nurture connections that bring positivity, understanding, and shared joy, where every soul feels nourished.

Prayer

Harmony Creator, bless my relationships. May they be sources of joy, understanding, and mutual support. May I not become so consumed with busyness that I miss out on the opportunities to be a friend. Amen.

DAY 79

CREATIVE EXPRESSION

Reflection

The language of the soul is expressed through creative expression. Today, reflect on the power of using creative outlets as a means of self-expression and rejuvenation. Let your creativity be a vibrant canvas for your emotions and thoughts.

Inspiration

In the act of creation, you breathe life into your innermost self. Whether through art, words, or movement, let creativity be the thread that weaves your unique story.

Prayer

Creative Spirit, awaken the muse within me. May my creative expressions be a reflection of my soul's journey and a source of rejuvenation. Amen.

DAY 80

DIVINE GUIDANCE

Reflection

Seeking and trusting in divine guidance is a journey of surrender and faith. Reflect on how you can open your heart to the whispers of the sacred, trusting that each step is guided by a higher purpose.

Inspiration

In the tapestry of life, divine guidance is the golden thread that weaves through every twist and turn. Trust in the guidance that leads you towards the extraordinary.

Prayer

Divine Guide, I surrender my path to you. I want a heart willing to be faithful to you in all seasons. Illuminate my journey with your wisdom, and may I trust in the unseen hands that guide me. Amen.

DAY 81

FORGIVENESS AND FREEDOM

Reflection

Embracing forgiveness is a path to personal freedom and healing. Reflect on the transformative power of letting go, allowing grace to wash over the wounds, and finding freedom in forgiveness. Release the weight of resentment and let the winds of grace carry you to a place of healing.

Inspiration

Forgiveness is looking at people with the spiritual knowledge of their innocence rather than the mortal perception of guilt.

Prayer

Source of Healing, Grant me the strength to forgive and the courage to release. May forgiveness be the key to the door of my personal freedom. Amen.

DAY 82

CELEBRATING PROGRESS

Reflection

Acknowledge and celebrate the small victories and progress on your journey. Reflect on the steps you've taken, no matter how small, and find joy in progressing toward a life of extraordinary living. Give yourself a treat!

Inspiration

In the dance of progress, every step is a celebration. Embrace the joy in the journey and honour the resilience that propels you forward.

Prayer

Joyful Creator, thank you for the progress made. May I find gratitude in each step and celebrate the journey towards extraordinary living. Amen.

DAY 83

GRACE IN IMPERFECTION

Reflection

Embrace grace and find beauty in imperfections. Reflect on the idea that perfection is not the goal but the journey of growth and the acceptance of your beautifully flawed self.

Inspiration

In the dance of imperfection, grace is the rhythm that makes each step meaningful. Embrace the beauty that arises when you let go of the pursuit of perfection.

Prayer

Graceful One, teach me to dance in the Light of imperfection. Be my Source of grace and strength to meet all the unknowns ahead. May I find beauty in my flaws and see the grace surrounding me. Amen.

DAY 84

SOULFUL REFLECTION

Reflection

Deepen your spiritual connection through introspective reflection. Take a moment to dive into the depths of your soul, exploring the quiet chambers where your true self resides. Today, spend some time in meditation.

Inspiration

In the stillness of reflection, the whispers of your soul become a gentle breeze. Dive deep, for in the soul's reflection, you discover the essence of your extraordinary being.

Prayer

Soulful Guide, lead me to the quiet waters of introspection. May I find clarity and connection in my soul's reflection depths.
Amen.

DAY 85

NOURISHING BODY AND SOUL

Reflection

Explore the connection between nutrition, self-care, and spiritual well-being. Reflect on how nourishing your body can be a sacred act that feeds the physical and spiritual.

Inspirational

Your body is a temple, and what you nourish it with shapes your spiritual landscape. Embrace a holistic approach to well-being, nurturing both body and soul.

Prayer

Sacred Source, bless my body with vitality and my soul with nourishment. May my choices reflect a reverence for the temple that houses my extraordinary spirit. Amen.

DAY 86

RADIANT ENERGY

Reflection

Cultivate positive energy and radiance through thoughts and actions. Reflect on the power of your energy, recognising that your thoughts and actions are like seeds that bloom into the garden of your life. Today, find three ways to infuse positive energy into your spirit.

Inspiration

Radiant energy is the Light that dispels darkness. Infuse positivity into your thoughts and actions, for you attract extraordinary possibilities in the glow of radiant energy.

Prayer

Radiant Light, fill me with positive energy. May my thoughts and actions be a beacon of Light, attracting positivity and illuminating the extraordinary path ahead. Amen.

DAY 87

LEGACY OF LOVE

Reflection

Reflect on the legacy of love you are creating and the impact on the lives of others. Acknowledge the ripple effect of your kindness, compassion, and love, for you leave an imprint on the world in the legacy of love.

Inspiration

Love is the eternal legacy that transcends time. Be mindful of the love you sow, for it blooms in the hearts of others, creating a legacy of extraordinary impact.

Prayer

Love Eternal, guide me in leaving a legacy of love. May my actions and words be seeds that blossom into a garden of compassion and kindness. Amen.

DAY 88

HARVESTING HOPE

Reflection
Focus on hope as a powerful force for extraordinary living. Reflect on the seeds of hope you've planted and the anticipation of a harvest that brings forth new beginnings and possibilities.

Inspiration
Hope is the sunrise after the darkest night. Cultivate the soil of your heart, for in the harvest of hope, you reap the extraordinary fruits of a resilient spirit.

Prayer
Hopeful Creator, bless the seeds of hope within me. May my heart be a fertile ground for the anticipation of new beginnings and the promise of a brighter tomorrow. Amen.

DAY 89

ACCESSORISING WITH FLEXIBILITY

Reflection

Flexibility is not just a physical attribute; it's the stylish accessory that complements the dance of life. How can you adorn yourself with the flexibility to navigate life's twists and turns gracefully?

Inspiration

Flexibility is the accessory that adds ease to your journey. Like a well-chosen scarf or tie, it enhances your style and allows you to adapt gracefully in every circumstance.

Prayer

Instructor of Life, help me master the stylish moves of flexibility. Grant me the flexibility to move with the rhythm of life. May I navigate the dance of life with the poise that comes from being adaptable.

DAY 90

"BLESSINGS AND BEGINNINGS"

Reflection

As you stand at the threshold of this day, reflect upon the remarkable journey you've undertaken. It's a tapestry woven with threads of resilience, faith, and the extraordinary moments that have shaped your path. ToDay is an invitation to marvel at the blessings received, both big and small, and to embrace the dawn of new beginnings.

Inspiration

In every closing chapter, there is a grace that unfolds. As you express gratitude for the journey, remember that each ending is a prelude to a new and exciting beginning. Life is a dance of appreciation and anticipation, a perpetual symphony of blessings and fresh starts.

Prayer

Gracious Guide, as I reflect on this journey, I'm grateful for the blessings woven into each day. In this moment of transition, grant me the wisdom to embrace the new beginnings awaiting me. May the tapestry of my life be adorned with the threads of gratitude and anticipation. Amen.

HOPE

DAY 91

AWAKENING PROSPERITY

Reflection

Today, awaken yourself to the abundant possibilities surrounding you. As you open your hearts to the richness of life, may you see the potential for prosperity in every moment.

Inspiration

Prosperity is not just about material wealth; it's a mindset that embraces the wealth of experiences, opportunities, and love life offers.

Prayer

Source of Abundance, Guide me in awakening to the prosperity that flows abundantly around me. May my mind be open to the richness of life, and may I recognise and appreciate the many forms of wealth that come my way. Amen.

DAY 92

ABUNDANCE ACTIVATION

Reflection

Gratitude unlocks the doors to prosperity. Today, activate the flow of abundance by acknowledging and appreciating the abundance already in your life.

Inspiration

In gratitude, we discover the true richness of life. It is the foundation upon which the abundance of the universe rests.

Prayer

Gracious Universe, As I activate the flow of abundance in my life, let gratitude be my constant companion. May my heart be a magnet for prosperity, drawing in the wealth of joy, love, and opportunities. Amen.

DAY 93

PROSPEROUS MINDSET AFFIRMATIONS

Reflection

Cultivate a mindset of prosperity through affirmations. Speak words of abundance and success into your life, creating a positive and empowering mental environment.

Inspiration

The words we speak to ourselves shape the reality we experience. Affirmations are the poetry of a prosperous mindset.

Prayer

Divine Architect of Thoughts,
Fashion my mind into a sanctuary of prosperity. May the affirmations I speak toDay lay the foundation for a life of success, joy, and abundance. Amen.

DAY 94

WEALTH VISUALISATION

Reflection

Envision the life of prosperity you desire. Allow your imagination to paint a vivid picture of wealth in all areas of your existence.

Inspiration

Visualisation is the brushstroke that paints our dreams into reality. Picture the life you wish to live and watch as the universe aligns to create it.

Prayer

Creative Force of the Universe,
Guide my thoughts as I embark on the canvas of my dreams. May the wealth I visualise manifest in my life, creating a masterpiece of prosperity. Amen.

DAY 95

FINANCIAL FREEDOM STRATEGIES

Reflection

Today, let's explore strategies for financial freedom. Empower yourself with the knowledge and wisdom to build a stable and secure financial future.

Inspiration

Financial freedom is the bridge that connects our dreams to reality. It begins with informed choices and disciplined actions.

Prayer

Divine Source of Wealth, bless me with the wisdom to make sound financial choices. May my actions align with the path to financial freedom, creating a secure foundation for an extraordinary life. Amen.

DAY 96

CAREER GROWTH REFLECTION

Reflection

Take a moment to reflect on your professional journey. What steps can you take toDay to nurture your career growth? Embrace the path of continuous improvement.

Inspiration

Your career is not just a set of different jobs; it's a canvas where you paint the masterpiece of your professional legacy.

Prayer

Guiding Star, illuminate my path as I reflect on my career. May each step be purposeful, each decision intentional, and each opportunity a stepping stone toward extraordinary professional fulfilment. Amen.

DAY 97

INVESTING IN SELF

Reflection

Your greatest asset is yourself. Consider how you can invest in your skills, knowledge, and well-being to enhance your personal and professional value.

Inspiration

Investing in oneself is the most rewarding investment, yielding dividends that extend beyond the boundaries of time.

Prayer

Divine Essence, grant me the wisdom to invest in myself. May the seeds of self-improvement blossom into a garden of expertise, resilience, and personal well-being. Amen.

DAY 98

GRATITUDE FOR FINANCIAL WELL-BEING

Reflection

Gratitude attracts abundance and opens the door to greater prosperity. Pause to express gratitude for your current financial well-being, no matter how small.

Inspiration

In the dance of prosperity, gratitude is the elegant waltz that leads to a symphony of abundance.

Prayer

Gracious Provider of Wealth, I offer gratitude for the financial well-being I experience. May my heart be a magnet for abundance, and may I use my resources to contribute to the well-being of others. Amen.

DAY 99

EMBRACING OPPORTUNITIES

Reflection

Opportunities are the threads that weave the tapestry of an extraordinary life. Look around you. Are there opportunities to embrace with an open heart and a learning readiness?

Inspiration

Life is a grand stage, and opportunities are the spotlight that illuminates our unique talents and potential.

Prayer

Opportunities Provider, guide me as I embrace the opportunities that come my way. May I approach each one with grace, courage, and a spirit of curiosity. Amen.

DAY 100

OPPORTUNITY MINDSET

Reflection

An opportunity mindset transforms challenges into stepping stones for growth. Today, reflect on cultivating a mindset that sees possibilities in every circumstance.

Inspiration

An opportunity mindset is a compass that directs us toward the hidden treasures within the challenges we face.

Prayer

Mindset Shaper, shape my thoughts into an opportunity mindset. May I see challenges as gateways to growth and setbacks as setups for comebacks. Amen.

DAY 101

NETWORKING FOR SUCCESS

Reflection

Reflect on the power of connections. How can intentional networking contribute to your journey of success? Today, consider building bridges that pave the way for extraordinary opportunities.

Inspiration

In the intricate dance of success, networking is the graceful waltz that connects dreams to reality.

Prayer

The orchestrator of Connections, guide me in creating meaningful connections on my path to success. May each interaction be a harmonious note in the symphony of my extraordinary journey. Amen.

DAY 102

SEIZING THE DAY

Reflection

ToDay is a gift. Each dawn brings a new canvas for you to paint the strokes of your extraordinary life. Make a commitment to seize the Day with enthusiasm and purpose.

Inspiration

In the tapestry of life, each Day is a unique thread. Seize it with intention, and your masterpiece will be extraordinary.

Prayer

Morning Light of Possibilities, illuminate my path as I seize the day. May my actions be purposeful, my spirit resilient, and my journey extraordinary. Amen.

DAY 103

INNOVATION AND CREATIVITY

Reflection

Reflect on the boundless power of innovation and creativity. How can you infuse these qualities into your endeavours, bringing uniqueness to your path of success?

Inspiration

Creativity is the gentle breeze that carries the fragrance of innovation. Let your ideas bloom into the extraordinary.

Prayer

Creative Spirit of Innovation, inspire my mind with creative brilliance. May my ideas be innovative, my creations extraordinary, and my journey marked by the elegance of originality. Amen.

DAY 104

BOLD DECISION-MAKING

Reflection

Bold decisions are the stepping stones to an extraordinary life. Reflect on embracing courage and decisiveness and considering their impact on your journey.

Inspiration

Be bold in your choices for decisions are the sculptor's tools, shaping the masterpiece of our destiny.

Prayer

Architect of Destiny, grant me the courage to make bold decisions. May each choice be a brushstroke that paints the canvas of my extraordinary life. Amen.

DAY 105

RISK-TAKING FOR SUCCESS

Reflection

Reflect on the relationship between risk and success. How can calculated risks propel you toward the extraordinary? Today, consider how you can embrace the adventure of stepping into the unknown.

Inspiration

In the daring dance of success, risk is the elegant partner that twirls us into the extraordinary.

Prayer

Brave Navigator of Destiny,
Guide me as I navigate the seas of uncertainty. May my calculated risks lead me to the shores of success, and may each challenge be a stepping stone to greatness.
Amen.

DAY 106

FUTURE SELF VISUALIZATION

Reflection

Envision the person you aspire to become. What qualities define your future self? Today, visualise, painting a vivid portrait of the extraordinary individual you are evolving into.

Inspiration

Visualisation is the artist's brush painting, the canvas of your destiny. Craft your future self with intention and watch the masterpiece of an extraordinary life unfold.

Prayer

Divine Atelier, bless my imagination as I visualise my future self. May the strokes of my aspirations create a portrait of an extraordinary life filled with purpose and grace. Amen.

DAY 107

VISION BOARD CREATION

Reflection

Take a moment to envision the life you desire. What dreams and aspirations fill your heart? Today, create your vision board, a visual manifesttation of your extraordinary future.

Inspiration

A vision board is a canvas where dreams and reality converge. Craft it with intention, and watch your extraordinary life unfold.

Prayer

Creative Source of Dreams, bless my hands as I craft my vision board. May each image and word be a brushstroke on the canvas of my destiny, creating a masterpiece of extraordinary living. Amen.

DAY 108

DAILY RITUALS FOR SUCCESS

Reflection

Reflect on the rituals that shape your daily life. What habits contribute to your success? Consider embracing daily rituals that align with your goals and cultivate a foundation for an extraordinary life.

Inspiration

Daily rituals are the stitches that weave the fabric of success. Thread them with intention and watch as your life becomes a tapestry of extraordinary achievements.

Prayer

Creator of Time and Routines, guide me in crafting daily rituals that lead to success. May each habit be a step towards the extraordinary, creating a life filled with purpose and accomplishment. Amen.

DAY 109

CELEBRATING MILESTONES

Reflection

Take a moment to reflect on the milestones you've achieved this year. Celebrate both the grand and the subtle victories along your journey. Each milestone is a testament to your resilience and progress.

Inspiration

In the symphony of life, milestones are the crescendos that add depth and richness to our melody. Celebrate your achievements, for they are the music of your extraordinary life."

Prayer

Divine Helper, I offer gratitude for the milestones I've reached. May each celebration be a note that resonates with the harmony of my extraordinary journey. Amen.

DAY 110

CULTIVATING BLISS

Reflection

Bliss is not just a destination but a journey in life's details. Today, reflect on the moments that bring you bliss and cultivate an awareness of the simple joys that elevate your spirit.

Inspiration

Bliss is the art of finding joy in the ordinary. Cultivate this art, and your life will be a masterpiece of extraordinary living.

Prayer

Creator of Joy, guide me as I cultivate bliss in my life. Open my eyes to find joy in the small moments and savour the sweetness of living an extraordinary life. Amen.

DAY 111

MINDFUL LIVING

Reflection

Mindful living is the key to unlocking the extraordinary within the ordinary. Consider the power of mindfulness in your daily life. How can being present in each moment enhance your experience?

Inspiration

In the gentle dance of mindfulness, every step becomes a celebration of life. Embrace the present with open arms and a receptive heart.

Prayer

Divine Presence, grant me the gift of mindfulness. May each moment be an opportunity to live fully, and may the ordinary be transformed into the extraordinary through mindful awareness. Amen.

DAY 112

JOYFUL HABITS

Reflection

Reflect on the habits that bring joy into your life. Consider cultivating practices that nurture your well-being, adding a touch of happiness to your daily routine.

Inspiration

Habits are the architects of our daily lives. Build joyful habits that construct a sanctuary of extraordinary living.

Prayer

Architect of Joyful Living, inspire me to build habits that bring joy into my daily life. May my routines be infused with the elegance of pleasure, creating a foundation for an extraordinary existence. Amen.

DAY 113

BLISSFUL RELATIONSHIPS

Reflection

Consider the relationships that bring bliss into your life. How can you nurture connections that uplift your spirit and contribute to the tapestry of your extraordinary journey?

Inspiration

Cultivate flowers of joy, understanding, and love in the garden of relationships. Let your connections be a source of bliss.

Prayer

Divine Connector, bless my connections with blissful energy. May my relationships reflect love, understanding, and joy, enriching my journey of extraordinary living. Amen.

DAY 114

EMPOWERING OTHERS

Reflection

Empowerment is a two-way street; as you uplift others, you create a ripple effect of extraordinary. Reflect on the power of empowering others. How can your actions lift those around you?

Inspiration

Empowering others is the silent symphony of impact. Each act of encouragement is a note that resonates in the hearts of many, creating a melody of extraordinary change.

Prayer

Divine Light, guide me in empowering those around me. May my words and actions be an uplifting melody, creating a harmonious rhythm of extraordinary change in the lives of others. Amen.

DAY 115

GRATITUDE FOR SIMPLE PLEASURES

Reflection

Reflect on the beauty of simplicity. What simple pleasures bring joy to your heart? Gratitude for these moments magnifies their significance, enriching the fabric of your extraordinary life.

Inspiration

In the garden of gratitude, simple pleasures bloom into extraordinary moments. Cherish the beauty in simplicity, for it holds the key to a life well-lived.

Prayer

Graceful Guardian, I express thanks for the simple pleasures that grace my life. I bless my surroundings, both the seen and the unseen. May my heart be a garden of gratitude, cultivating joy in the smallest moments.
Amen.

DAY 116

PURSUING PASSIONS

Reflection

Pursuing your passions is a journey towards the extraordinary, as it aligns your heart with your purpose. Contemplate the passions that ignite your soul. What activities bring you alive?

Inspiration

Passions are the whispers of the soul calling us to live authentically. Embrace your passions, for they are the compass guiding you to an extraordinary life.

Prayer

Soul Navigator, guide me as I pursue the desires of my heart. May my passions be a tapestry woven with threads of purpose, creating a life rich with meaning and extraordinary moments. Amen.

DAY 117

INNER HARMONY

Reflection

Cultivating inner peace and balance is the foundation of an extraordinary life. Reflect on the harmony within. How can you align your mind, body, and spirit to create this harmony?

Inspiration

In the symphony of life, inner harmony is the melody that soothes the soul. Tune into the music within and dance to the rhythm of your extraordinary existence.

Prayer

Divine peace, grant me the serenity to cultivate inner harmony. May my thoughts, actions, and spirit harmonise to create a symphony of peace within me. Amen.

DAY 118

NATURE'S BLISS

Reflection

Nature's bliss is a balm for the soul, providing solace and inspiration. Spend a moment in nature, observing its beauty. How can you integrate the tranquillity of nature into your daily life?

Inspiration

Nature whispers secrets of tranquillity and joy. Let its blissful embrace remind you of the extraordinary beauty that surrounds you.

Prayer

Creator of the Universe, I seek refuge in the bliss of nature. May its serenity infuse my spirit, and may I find joy in the simple yet profound beauty of the world around me.
Amen.

DAY 119

SELF-REFLECTION

Reflection

Self-awareness is the compass that guides you on the extraordinary journey of self-discovery. Set aside time for self-reflection. Delve into the depths of your thoughts and emotions.

Inspiration

In the mirror of self-reflection, we discover the extraordinary within. Dive deep, for the reflections you find will be the treasures of your soul.

Prayer

Divine Light, illuminate the corridors of my inner self. May self-reflection be a mirror that reveals the extraordinary potential within me, guiding me on the path of authenticity. Amen.

DAY 120

CELEBRATION OF EXTRAORDINARY LIVING

Reflection

Take a moment to reflect on the extraordinary journey of your life. Consider the paths you've walked, the challenges you've overcome, and the moments that have filled your heart with joy. In this reflection, let gratitude for the tapestry of your experiences guide your thoughts.

Inspiration

The celebration of extraordinary living is not found in the grandiose events alone but in acknowledging the beauty woven into the fabric of our daily existence. Embrace each thread, for it contributes to the extraordinary masterpiece of your life.

Prayer

Eternal Creator, I offer gratitude for the extraordinary moments that have graced my journey. May my heart be adorned with the elegance of appreciation, and may I celebrate the richness of life with grace and joy. Amen.

DAY 121

ROOTS OF HUMILITY

Reflection

Today, explore the roots from which your humility springs. What experiences and lessons have shaped your understanding of humility?

Inspiration

Humility begins with acknowledging our origins. Embrace the richness of your roots, for they provide the foundation for growth and humility.

Prayer

Gracious Creator, help me to honour and draw strength from the roots of my being. May my humility reflect the depth and authenticity within me. Amen.

DAY 122

THE DANCE OF HUMILITY

Reflection

Consider humility as a dance: graceful, intentional, and harmonious. How can you move through life with the elegance of humility?

Inspiration

Every step in the dance of humility is a gesture of respect and understanding. Embrace the rhythm of humility in your interactions.

Prayer

Divine Choreographer, guide my steps in the dance of humility. May my steps reflect grace, understanding, and a genuine respect for others. Amen.

DAY 123

ELEVATED BY HUMILITY

Reflection

Reflect on moments when humility has lifted you to new heights. How has embracing humility elevated your character and relationships?

Inspiration

True elevation comes not from arrogance but from the wings of humility. Soar to new heights, knowing humility is the wind beneath your wings.

Prayer

Heavenly Elevator, lift me higher through the virtue of humility. May I ascend with grace, acknowledging that true greatness lies in humility. Amen.

DAY 124

THE ART OF LISTENING

Reflection

Explore the art of active listening today. How can you deepen your understanding of others through the gift of attentive ears?

Inspiration

Listening is an art that paints understanding, compassion, and humility onto the canvas of our relationships.

Prayer

Wise Listener, grant me the ability to hear words and the more profound melodies of others' hearts. In listening, may I find the beauty of humility. Amen.

DAY 125

THE HUMBLE LEADER

Reflection

Contemplate the qualities of a humble leader. How can you embody leadership that inspires and uplifts?

Inspiration

A humble leader is like a gentle breeze, felt but never seen. Lead with humility, and you will leave an indelible mark on hearts.

Prayer

Guiding Light, illuminate my path as a humble leader. May my leadership inspire others to rise and shine, fostering a culture of humility. Amen.

DAY 126

HUMILITY IN ADVERSITY

Reflection

Consider times when adversity has tested your humility. How did humility become a source of strength during these times?

Inspiration

Adversity is the forge where humility is refined into strength. In the face of challenges, let humility be your shield and sword.

Prayer

Divine Spirit, fortify me with the armour of humility in times of adversity. May challenges be the canvas where my humility paints a masterpiece. Amen.

DAY 127

ACTS OF KINDNESS

Reflection

Reflect on the power of kindness. How have acts of kindness shaped your life? Today, consider the impact of simple, intentional gestures that uplift others and create a ripple effect of positivity.

Inspiration

Kindness is the language of the extraordinary soul. In each act, we compose a symphony of compassion that reverberates far beyond our immediate reach.

Prayer

Compassionate God, may my actions be notes in the grand symphony of kindness. Guide me to perform acts of grace that resonate with the melody of an extraordinary life. Amen.

DAY 128

PURITY OF PURPOSE

Reflection

Delve into the depths of your purpose. How can aligning your actions with a pure purpose enhance the quality of your life?

Inspiration

Purpose infused with purity is a guiding light, illuminating the path to a more meaningful and fulfilling existence.

Prayer

Divine Illuminator, reveal to me the pure essence of my purpose. May my actions be aligned with the radiant clarity of a purposeful heart. Amen.

DAY 129

RADIANT PURITY

Reflection

Envision your life as a canvas painted with radiant purity. What colours and brushstrokes define the beauty of your pure existence?

Inspiration

Radiant purity is the masterpiece of a life lived authentically. Let your inner light shine, casting a luminous glow on the world.

Prayer

Creator of Life, paint my life with the vibrant hues of radiant purity. May my existence be a masterpiece that inspires and uplifts. Amen.

DAY 130

PURITY IN PROGRESS

Reflection

Acknowledge the journey of becoming purer. How can you celebrate your progress while embracing your ongoing refinement?

Inspiration

Purity is a perpetual journey, not a destination. Celebrate each step forward, for progress is a testament to your commitment.

Prayer

Eternal Guide, accompany me on this journey of purity. May I find joy in the process, knowing each step forward is a victory. Amen.

DAY 131

THE SYMPHONY OF PURITY

Reflection

Consider how various aspects of your life harmonize where there's purity. What melodies can you create by orchestrating pure intentions in everything you do?

Inspiration

The symphony of purity is a melody that resonates through every thought, action, and relationship. Let your life be a harmonious composition.

Prayer

Maestro of Life, guide me in composing the symphony of purity. May the notes of my intentions create a masterpiece of grace and virtue. Amen.

DAY 132

PURITY OF THE MIND

Reflection

Reflect on the cleanliness of your mind. How can you cleanse it from negativity and cultivate thoughts of purity?

Inspiration

A pure mind is a sanctuary of serenity. Sweep away the dust of negativity, leaving a space adorned with the purity of uplifting thoughts.

Prayer

Divine Purifier, purify my mind from the clutter of negativity. May my thoughts be a source of inspiration and joy. Amen.

DAY 133

PURITY IN ACTION

Reflection

Explore how your actions can be expressions of purity. In what ways can you infuse purity into your daily deeds and interactions?

Inspiration

Purity in action is a dance of grace and kindness. Let your every step be a testament to the elegance of a pure heart in motion.

Prayer

Guiding Light, illuminate my actions with the purity of intention. May my deeds create ripples of goodness in the world. Amen.

DAY 134

PURITY'S REFLECTION

Reflection

Look into the mirror of purity. What reflections do you see? How does purity shape the image you present to the world?

Inspiration

Purity's reflection is the most authentic image of the soul. Embrace the beauty it reveals, for you find the essence of your authentic self in purity.

Prayer

Divine Illuminator, show me the reflection of my soul through the lens of purity. May my presence be a testament to the beauty within. Amen.

DAY 135

THE PROTECTIVE PRESENCE

Reflection

Reflect on the protective presence that surrounds you. What does it feel like to be embraced by the warmth and security of a divine guardian?

Inspiration

In the protective presence, you find solace and courage. Allow yourself to bask in the reassuring light of divine guardianship.

Prayer

Guardian of Grace, envelop me in your protective presence. May I find strength and comfort in the shelter of your unwavering love. Amen.

DAY 136

SEEKING REFUGE

Reflection

Reflect on times you sought shelter from life's storms. How did finding Refuge impact your resilience and ability to face challenges?

Inspiration

Seeking Refuge is not a sign of weakness but a testament to your wisdom. Embrace the sanctuaries that nurture and replenish your spirit.

Prayer

Divine Refuge guide me to the havens of peace and strength. Grant me the courage to seek Refuge when storms arise.

DAY 137

NOURISHED BY DIVINE LOVE

Reflection

Contemplate the nourishing power of divine love. How does divine love sustain and replenish you in your journey?

Inspiration

Love is a bountiful feast for the soul. Allow yourself to be nourished by the unconditional love surrounding you.

Prayer

Source of Love, fill my cup with the nectar of your unconditional affection. May I be forever nourished and sustained by Your love that surrounds me.

DAY 138

NURTURING SELF-CARE

Reflection

Explore the concept of self-care as a form of nurturing. Reflect on how you can cultivate a practice of self-care that honours and uplifts your being?

Inspiration

Nurturing self-care is a sacred ritual that replenishes your spirit. Honour yourself with the care and attention you deserve.

Prayer

Divine Caregiver, teach me the art of nurturing self-care. May I lavish myself with the kindness and attention that nurtures my soul.

DAY 139

HEALTHY BOUNDARIES

Reflection

Reflect on the role of healthy boundaries in your life. How can setting and honouring boundaries be an act of self-love?

Inspiration

Healthy boundaries are bridges to self-respect and harmony. Set boundaries with love, recognising the sanctity of your own space.

Prayer

Wise Protector, guide me in setting healthy boundaries. May I navigate relationships with grace, honouring both myself and others.

DAY 140

GUARDIANSHIP OF THE HEART

Reflection

Contemplate the guardianship of your heart. How can you protect and nurture the tender core of your being?

Inspiration

The guardianship of the heart is a sacred duty. Fortify your heart with love, wisdom, and resilience against life's challenges.

Prayer

Guardian of my Heart, shield my tender core from negativity. May the beat of my heart resonate with the rhythm of love and courage.

DAY 141

THE STRENGTH OF VULNERABILITY

Reflection

Consider the strength found in vulnerability. How has embracing vulnerability empowered you in your relationships and personal growth?

Inspiration

Vulnerability is the birthplace of strength. Embrace the power that comes from revealing your authentic self to the world.

Prayer

Divine Spirit, grant me the courage to be vulnerable. Give me the strength and the authenticity to become a beacon of light for others. Amen.

DAY 142

HARMONY OF HUMILITY, PURITY, AND PROTECTION

Reflection

Reflect on the harmony of humility, purity, and protection. How do these virtues intertwine to create a symphony of grace in your life?

Inspiration

You find the sweet melody of an extraordinary life in the harmony of virtues. Embrace the exquisite balance they bring to your journey.

Prayer

Divine Harmony, weave the threads of humility, purity, and protection into the fabric of my life. May their symphony create a masterpiece of grace and resilience. Amen.

DAY 143

WHOLENESS WITHIN

Reflection
Explore the concept of wholeness within; what does this mean to you? Reflect on the aspects of your being contributing to your sense of completeness.

Inspiration
Wholeness is not the absence of flaws but the acceptance and integration of every facet of your being. Embrace the completeness that resides within you.

Prayer
Sacred Centre, help me recognise and embrace the wholeness within me. May I walk the path of self-acceptance with grace and gratitude. Amen.

DAY 144

EMPOWERED BY VIRTUE

Reflection

Reflect on the empowering nature of virtue. How do virtues empower you to navigate challenges and make meaningful choices?

Inspiration

Virtue is the source of true empowerment. Allow the virtues of kindness, integrity, and love to guide your actions and decisions.

Prayer

Source of Virtue, empower me with the strength of integrity and the warmth of compassion. May I navigate life's journey with grace and purpose. Amen.

DAY 145

LUMINOUS LIVING

Reflection

Take time to reflect on the idea of luminous living. How can you infuse your life with the brilliance of joy, love, and purpose?

Inspiration

Luminous living is a choice to radiate positivity and embrace the beauty of every moment. Shine brightly, and let your light illuminate the world.

Prayer

Divine Light, guide me to live a luminous life. May my presence brighten the lives of those around me, creating a tapestry of joy and love. Amen.

DAY 146

GRATITUDE FOR CHALLENGES

Reflection

Consider the challenges you've faced. How have they shaped your character and resilience? Today, express gratitude for the lessons and growth that challenges bring; they are stepping stones to the extraordinary.

Inspiration

Challenges are the sculptors of our strength. Embrace them with gratitude, for the seeds of extraordinary resilience lie within their folds.

Prayer

Divine Help, I offer gratitude for the challenges I've encountered. May my spirit be as resilient as marble, shaped into an extraordinary masterpiece through life's sculpting challenges. Amen.

DAY 147

ETERNAL ECHOES

Reflection

Reflect on the echoes of your actions and choices. How do you want your life to resonate in the hearts and minds of others?

Inspiration

Your actions create eternal echoes, reverberating through time. Choose a path that leaves a legacy of kindness, love, and inspiration.

Prayer

Eternal Presence, help me make choices that create positive echoes. May my life be a melody of love and compassion that resonates through eternity. Amen.

DAY 148

SACRED BALANCE

Reflection

Contemplate the importance of maintaining sacred balance in your life. How can you achieve equilibrium between different aspects of your journey?

Inspiration

Balance is the art of harmonising opposing forces. Strive for a sacred balance that nurtures your mind, body, and soul.

Prayer

Divine Peace, guide me in finding and maintaining a sacred balance in my life. May I walk the tightrope of existence with elegance and poise. Amen.

DAY 149

LIVING GRACEFULLY

Reflection

Reflect on the concept of living gracefully. How can you move through life with ease, gratitude, and kindness?

Inspiration

Living gracefully is an art that involves dancing through challenges with gratitude and embracing each step of the journey.

Prayer

Divine Grace, teach me the dance of living with elegance. May I move through life with gratitude, kindness, and an open heart.
Amen.

DAY 150

RADIANT SPIRIT

Reflection

Contemplate the radiance of your spirit. Explore ways to nurture and let your inner light shine even brighter.

Inspiration

Your spirit is a radiant force that can light up the darkest corners. Allow your inner light to shine with unapologetic brilliance.

Prayer

Luminous Spirit, infuse me with the courage to let my light shine. May my spirit radiate love, joy, and kindness, illuminating the path for myself and others. Amen.

DAY 151

LEGACY REFLECTION

Reflection

Consider the legacy you wish to leave. What values and actions define the legacy you want to be remembered for? Reflecting on your legacy shapes the extraordinary impact you have on the world.

Inspiration

Legacy is the echo of your existence in the hearts of others. Craft a legacy that resonates with the beauty of kindness, love, and purpose.

Prayer

Eternal One, guide me as I reflect on the legacy I am creating. May my actions be imbued with grace, and may my legacy be a testament to a life of purpose and extraordinary love. Amen.

DAY 152

FOUNDATIONS OF LOVE

Reflection

In the tapestry of life, Love forms the foundation, weaving connections that endure. Reflect on the roots of your capacity to love and the relationships shaping your journey. What does this feel like?

Inspiration

Love is the bedrock of a life well-lived. As you build upon the foundation of Love, let its strength guide you through every twist and turn.

Prayer

Divine source of Love, bless me with the wisdom to nurture and cherish the foundations of Love in my life. May my heart be a sanctuary for compassion and understanding. Amen.

DAY 153

SELF-LOVE AFFIRMATIONS

Reflection

Look in the mirror of self-reflection. Affirm your worth, acknowledging the beauty within. Today, let self-love be the melody that orchestrates your thoughts and actions. You deserve a treat!

Inspiration

Self-love is the symphony that harmonises the soul. As you affirm your worth, you compose a life that resonates with confidence and joy.

Prayer

Eternal Love, as I affirm my worth and embrace the beauty within, may self-love illuminate my path, casting out doubt and welcoming the light of confidence. Amen.

DAY 154

GRATITUDE FOR LOVE AND BEAUTY

Reflection

Take a moment to reflect on the profound blessings of Love and beauty in your life. Consider the people, moments, and experiences that have filled your heart with Love and your surroundings with beauty. How has the intertwining of Love and beauty enriched your journey?

Inspiration

Love and beauty are the exquisite threads that weave the fabric of our existence. In gratitude, recognise the extraordinary living that emerges from the harmonious dance of these divine elements.

Prayer

Divine Beauty, I bow in gratitude for the precious gifts that grace my life. May my heart be a sanctuary for Love, and may my eyes be open to the exquisite beauty surrounding me. May I find the true essence of extraordinary living in moments of gratitude. Amen.

DAY 155

UNCONDITIONAL LOVE

Reflection

Unconditional Love knows no bounds or limitations. Reflect on the expansiveness of your heart. How can you cultivate a limitless love, embracing both imperfections and strengths?

Inspiration

Unconditional Love is the gentle breeze that carries us through life's storms. Embrace the boundless nature of Love, and let it be your guiding light.

Prayer

Divine source of Love, teach me to love without conditions. May my heart be a haven of acceptance, embracing the beauty in every soul. Amen.

DAY 156

LOVE LANGUAGES

Reflection

Discover the poetry of connection by understanding your love languages. Reflect on the unique dialects that resonate within your heart and the hearts of those you cherish. What can you learn?

Inspiration

Love languages are the sweet whispers that resonate in the language of the heart. Today, speak and listen in the dialect of Love that nourishes your soul.

Prayer

Guiding spirit of Love, help me understand and honour the unique languages of Love. May my relationships flourish as I learn to express and receive Love in various forms.
Amen.

DAY 157

FAMILY BONDS

Reflection

Family is the tapestry of our shared stories, woven with threads of love. Reflect on the beauty of family bonds and their unique role in shaping your beautiful life.

Inspiration

Family bonds are the treasures that enrich our journey. Today, honour the ties that bind you and let the love within your family radiate brightly.

Prayer

Eternal Glory, bless my relatives with love and understanding. May our bonds be strong, our hearts be connected, and our journey be graced with the beauty of family. Amen.

DAY 158

FRIENDSHIP FOREVER

Reflection

Friendship is a garden of shared laughter and shared tears. Reflect on the friendships that have beautified your life. How have these connections shaped your journey, and how can you nurture them today?

Inspiration

Friendship is a timeless melody that echoes through the corridors of our hearts. Embrace the joy of camaraderie and let the symphony of true friendship be your life's soundtrack.

Prayer

Eternal Source of Friendship, bless my bonds with the grace of enduring connection. May my heart be a sanctuary for genuine companionship, and may the tapestry of friendship weave richness into my life. Amen.

DAY 159

ROMANTIC GESTURES

Reflection

Romance is the art of weaving magic into the ordinary. Reflect on the romantic gestures that have graced your life. How can you infuse your Day with enchantment and express love through thoughtful acts?

Inspiration

Romance is the poetry of the heart, written in gestures that dance with emotion. Today, let your actions be verses of love, creating a tapestry of romance in the mundane.

Prayer

Creator of Romance, guide my hands and heart in crafting gestures of love. May my actions speak volumes, and may the tapestry of romance unfurl in the everyDay moments of my life. Amen.

DAY 160

GRATITUDE FOR LOVE

Reflection

Gratitude is the golden thread that binds hearts together. Reflect on the love that surrounds you. How can you express gratitude for the love you've received and cultivate an attitude of thankfulness?

Inspiration

Gratitude is the heartbeat of a life well-lived. Today, let your heart sing with appreciation for the love that weaves through the fabric of your existence.

Prayer

Gracious Source of Love, thank you for Your love that envelops my life. May my gratitude be as boundless as the love I receive, and may it radiate in all directions. Amen.

DAY 161

BEAUTY THEMES

Reflection

Beauty is the silent poet that speaks to the soul. Reflect on the beauty that surrounds you. How can you create aesthetic wonders that enrich your daily experience?

Inspiration

Beauty is a language the heart understands. Today, immerse yourself in the exquisite poetry of your surroundings and let beauty be your guide.

Prayer

Divine Atelier, open my eyes to the wonders that adorn my world. May I find inspiration in the elegance around me and reflect that beauty in my thoughts and actions. Amen.

DAY 162

INNER BEAUTY

Reflection

Inner beauty, the radiant glow that transcends appearances. Reflect on the qualities within yourself that radiate beauty. How can you nurture and share this inner radiance with the world?

Inspiration

Inner beauty is the timeless elegance that leaves an indelible mark on the soul. Today, celebrate the qualities within you that make your heart shine with grace.

Prayer

Soulful Source of Beauty, guide me in cultivating the inner radiance that defines true beauty. May my actions be adorned with kindness, compassion, and the timeless elegance of a beautiful soul. Amen.

DAY 163

NATURE'S BEAUTY

Reflection

Nature's beauty is a masterpiece painted with the colours of serenity. Reflect on the beauty of the natural world. How can you connect with and appreciate the tranquillity found in nature?

Inspiration

Nature's beauty is a serene symphony that soothes the soul. Today, take a moment to immerse yourself in the artistry of the world around you and find solace in its beauty.

Prayer

Creator of Nature, bless me with the wisdom to appreciate the tranquillity of your creations. May the beauty of nature inspire peace within my heart. Amen.

DAY 164

CREATIVE EXPRESSION

Reflection

Creativity, the vibrant dance of imagination and expression. Reflect on the ways you express your creativity. How can you infuse your Day with artistic flair and let your unique creativity shine?

Inspiration

Creative expression is the art of the soul, a dance that celebrates individuality. Today, let your creativity flow freely, painting the canvas of your life with bold and beautiful strokes.

Prayer

Divine Spirit of Creativity, guide my hands and heart in expressing the unique masterpiece of my soul. May my creative endeavours reflect the beauty within. Amen.

DAY 165

FINDING BEAUTY IN DIVERSITY

Reflection

Diversity is the vibrant palette that paints the tapestry of humanity. Reflect on the beauty found in our differences. How can you embrace diversity and see the unique beauty in every soul you encounter?

Inspiration

Diversity is the kaleidoscope of life, each unique hue contributing to the masterpiece of our shared existence. Today, open your heart to the beauty of diversity in the rich tapestry.

Prayer

Sovereign Creator, grant me the wisdom to appreciate the beauty in every shade and form. May my heart be a sanctuary for unity, and my actions reflect the reverence for the diverse beauty surrounding me. Amen.

DAY 166

BEAUTY IN SIMPLICITY

Reflection

Simplicity, the elegant artistry of uncomplicated moments. Reflect on the beauty found in simplicity. How can you pare down the complexities of life to reveal the pure and exquisite beauty hidden within the ordinary?

Inspiration

Simplicity is the canvas upon which true beauty paints its masterpiece. Today, seek the beauty in simplicity and let the elegance of uncluttered moments enrich your soul.

Prayer

Architect of Simplicity, guide me in appreciating the beauty that lies in the uncomplicated. May my heart be attuned to the elegance of simplicity, and may my actions reflect this refined beauty. Amen.

DAY 167

REDISCOVERING ROMANCE

Reflection

Pause and reflect on the romance that may have faded into the background. What are the unique elements that once defined the romance in your life? How can you rediscover and reignite those sparks?

Inspiration

Romance is the art of making the ordinary extraordinary. Today, commit to rediscovering the subtle nuances that breathe life into romance and let the embers of Love glow anew.

Prayer

Divine Love, guide me in rediscovering the melody of Love. May my heart be attuned to the subtle melodies of romance surrounding me, turning everyDay moments into poetic expressions of Love. Amen.

DAY 168

REDISCOVERING PASSION

Reflection

Reflect on the passion that once fuelled your pursuits and relationships. What aspects of your life could benefit from a renewed sense of passion? How can you reignite the flames of enthusiasm and fervour?

Inspiration

Passion is the heartbeat of a purposeful life. Today, seek out the embers of passion within and let the fire of enthusiasm illuminate your path to extraordinary living.

Prayer

Divine Source of Inspiration, reignite the flames of zeal within my heart. May my pursuits and relationships be fuelled by the energy of passion, infusing each of my endeavours with purpose and vibrancy. Amen.

DAY 169

CULTIVATING ROMANCE IN EVERYDAY LIFE

Reflection

Consider how you can infuse daily routines with romantic touches. What small gestures can you incorporate to create an atmosphere of Love and connection amid the ordinary?

Inspiration

Romance need not be reserved for special occasions. Today, let every breath be a love note and every gesture a dance of romance, turning the ordinary into the extraordinary.

Prayer

Creator of Romance, teach me the art of infusing everyDay moments with Love. May my actions and words be a testament to the enduring beauty of romance in the tapestry of my daily life. Amen.

DAY 170

GRATITUDE FOR ROMANCE

Reflection

Pause and reflect on the romance that colours your life. Consider the moments of tenderness, shared laughter, and the subtle gestures that speak volumes. How has romance added a layer of beauty to your days, and what unique qualities does it bring to your relationship?

Inspiration

Romance is the poetic rhythm that dances through the symphony of Love. Today, reflect on the magic that romance has woven into the fabric of your relationship. In each romantic note, find a verse of gratitude, celebrating the fantastic dance of hearts.

Prayer

Lover of my Soul, I am grateful for the enchanting presence of Love in my life. May the tapestry of romance continue to unfold, weaving moments of beauty and joy into the narrative of our relationship. Bless our journey with an abundance of Love and grace. Amen.

DAY 171

GRATITUDE FOR BEAUTY

Reflection

Gratitude is the golden key that unlocks the door to a life well-lived. Reflect on the beauty for which you are grateful. How can you express your appreciation for the beauty that graces your life?

Inspiration

Gratitude is the sweet melody that accompanies the dance of beauty. Today, let your heart sing with appreciation, and may your gratitude be a testament to the beauty that enriches your days.

Prayer

Generous Giver of Beauty, I am grateful for the exquisite moments that colour my life. May my heart be a vessel of thanks, and may my actions reflect my deep appreciation for the beauty around me. Amen.

DAY 172

ROMANCE THEMES

Reflection

Romance, the dance of hearts intertwined. Reflect on the romance that enriches your life. How can you infuse your relationships with the passion, tenderness, and enchantment characterising a romantic spirit?

Inspiration

Romance is the poetry that elevates Love to its highest form. Today, let the spirit of romance illuminate your connections, and may the dance of hearts leave an indelible mark on your journey.

Prayer

Eternal One, bless my relationships with the magic of tenderness and passion. May the flame of romance burn brightly, turning each moment into a poetic dance of Love. Amen.

DAY 173

DATE NIGHT IN

Reflection

Reflect on the "Date Night In" concept and the intimacy it can foster. How can you create a cosy and romantic atmosphere within the comfort of your own home? What activities can you share to deepen your connection?

Inspiration

Home is where the heart is; tonight, let it be the canvas for a date night. Rediscover the joy of shared moments, laughter, and the simple beauty of being together.

Prayer

Creator of Home and Hearth, bless this space with the warmth of Love. May our date night be filled with laughter, connection, and the shared intimacy that strengthens the bond of Love. Amen.

DAY 174

NURTURING INTIMACY

Reflection

Contemplate the depth of intimacy in your relationships. How can you nurture a sense of closeness and vulnerability? What actions can you take to foster a deeper connection with your loved ones?

Inspiration

Intimacy is the tender dance of souls connecting. Today, open your heart to vulnerability and nurture the sacred space where true intimacy flourishes.

Prayer

Guardian of my Soul, guide me in nurturing the sacred bond between hearts. May my actions reflect the deep Love and connection that form the foundation of intimate relationships. Amen.

DAY 175

THE ART OF COMMUNICATION

Reflection

Take a moment to reflect on the profound impact of communication in your life. How have your words and expressions shaped your relationships, both positively and negatively? Consider the beauty that emerges when communication is thoughtful, clear, and empathetic.

Inspiration

Communication is the brushstroke that paints the canvas of our connections. Today, recognise the artistry within your words and gestures. Let them be strokes of kindness, understanding, and grace, creating a masterpiece of meaningful connections.

Prayer

Eloquent Creator of Words, bless my communication with the artistry of kindness. May my words be a tapestry of understanding, my gestures be strokes of empathy, and my silence be a canvas for listening. Guide me in the art of communication, creating a symphony of harmony in my relationships. Amen.

DAY 176

ADVENTURE TOGETHER

Reflection

Contemplate the beauty of embarking on an adventure together. How does the shared journey strengthen your connection and create lasting memories? Reflect on the excitement and joy that come from exploring life hand-in-hand.

Inspiration

Life is an adventure waiting to be explored, and together, it becomes a tapestry of shared moments and mutual discovery. Today, celebrate the thrill of your shared journey and the extraordinary experiences that lie ahead.

Prayer

Divine Love, bless our journey with excitement and discovery. May our adventures deepen our bond and infuse our lives with the extraordinary. Amen.

DAY 177

ROMANTIC MEMORIES

Reflection

Reflect on cherished romantic memories. What moments stand out as eternally unique in your shared history? Allow the warmth of those memories to fill your heart with gratitude and love.

Inspiration

Romantic memories are the jewels of our shared history, glistening with the beauty of love. Today, treasure the moments that have woven a tapestry of romance, creating a legacy of love.

Prayer

Creator of Life, thank you for the romantic moments that grace our shared history. May these memories be a source of joy and inspiration, reminding us of the beauty we've created together. Amen.

DAY 178

ROMANTIC GESTURES

Reflection

Consider the power of small romantic gestures. How do these tender actions speak volumes of love? Reflect on the beauty found in expressing affection through thoughtful and intentional acts.

Inspiration

Romantic gestures are the poetry of love, written in the language of actions. Today, let your gestures be sonnets, expressing the depth of your love in elegant simplicity.

Prayer

Masterful Composer of Romance, guide my actions to become notes in the symphony of love. May my gestures be a melodic expression of affection, filling our lives with the beauty of romance. Amen."

DAY 179

LOVE & BEAUTY RITUALS

Reflection

Contemplate the role of love and beauty rituals in your relationship. How do shared rituals enhance your connection and create a sense of harmony? Reflect on the importance of intentional moments that celebrate love.

Inspiration

Love and beauty rituals are the sacred dances of our connection, choreographed with intention and grace. Today, celebrate the rituals that infuse your relationship with the divine.

Prayer

Artisan of Love and Beauty, bless our shared rituals with depth and meaning. May the intentional moments we create become expressions of our love, enhancing the beauty surrounding us. Amen.

DAY 180

ROMANTIC GETAWAYS (IMAGINARY OR REAL)

Reflection

Imagine or reminisce about romantic getaways, whether real or in dreams. How do these moments of escape enrich your relationship? Reflect on the importance of creating spaces for shared adventure and relaxation.

Inspiration

Romantic getaways, whether real or imagined, are the breaths of fresh air that rejuvenate our love. Today, let your mind wander to dreamy destinations or plan a getaway to nurture your connection.

Prayer

Architect of Romantic Escapes, guide us in creating moments of retreat and joy. May our getaways, whether in reality or fantasy, be a source of renewal and inspiration for our love. Amen."

DAY 181

ACTS OF LOVE AND BEAUTY FOR OTHERS

Reflection

Reflect on the transformative power of extending acts of love and beauty beyond your relationship. How do these gestures create a ripple effect, spreading joy and kindness to others? Contemplate the beauty found in giving.

Inspiration

Acts of love and beauty for others echo our shared grace reverberating in the world. Today, consider how your kindness can illuminate the lives of those around you.

Prayer

Benevolent Source of Love and Beauty, inspire me to be a conduit of kindness. May my acts of love and beauty create a ripple effect, touching the hearts of others and enhancing the extraordinary in their lives.
Amen.

DAY 182

GRACIOUS BEGINNINGS

Reflection
Begin toDay with a heart open to grace. Consider the moments in your life where grace has embraced you, allowing you to move forward with an unburdened spirit.

Inspiration
In the dance of life, let grace be your partner. With each step, embrace the rhythm of kindness, and let your journey be a masterpiece of gracious beginnings.

Prayer
Dear Source, grace me with the strength to begin each Day with gratitude, forgiveness, and an open heart. May my journey be adorned with the elegance of kindness. Amen.

DAY 183

VISION FOR EXTRAORDINARY LIVING

Reflection

In the sanctuary of your thoughts, contemplate the vision you hold for your life, which transcends the ordinary and reaches for the extraordinary. What dreams and aspirations reside in the canvas of your imagination? How can you craft a vision that becomes the guiding star on your journey to exceptional living?

Inspiration

A vision is the brushstroke that paints the canvas of our destiny. It is the compass that directs our steps toward extraordinary living. Today, allow your imagination to soar, envisioning a life filled with purpose, passion, and the exquisite beauty of your dreams.

Prayer

Artistic Creator of Visions, bless me with the clarity to envision a life of extraordinary beauty and purpose. May my dreams be vibrant strokes on the canvas of my destiny, and may my vision illuminate the path to extraordinary living. Guide me in manifesting the special in every facet of my existence. Amen.

DAY 184

EXTRAORDINARY LIVING MANIFESTO

Reflection

In the stillness of this moment, reflect on your life journey. Contemplate the desires that stir in your heart, the dreams that dance in your imagination, and the extraordinary possibilities that await. What does extraordinary living mean to you? How can you craft a personal manifesto that embodies the essence of your unique journey?

Inspiration

An Extraordinary Living Manifesto is the anthem of the soul, a declaration that resonates with the rhythm of your dreams. It is the compass guiding you towards a life of purpose, passion, and profound fulfilment. Today, fashion a manifesto that ignites the spark of extraordinary living within you.

Prayer

Visionary Creator, as I pen the chapters of my Extraordinary Living Manifesto, grant me the wisdom to articulate my soul's desires. May each word declare purpose, and may the manifesto become a guiding light, leading me to a life of extraordinary beauty and meaning. Amen.

DAY 185

INNER HARMONY

Reflection

Amidst the ebb and flow of life's symphony, find a moment to reflect on inner harmony. Consider the various elements within yourself, the notes of your emotions, the rhythm of your thoughts, and the melodies of your aspirations. How can you attune them to create a harmonious masterpiece?

Inspiration

Inner harmony is the exquisite dance of alignment within your soul. It is the art of orchestrating the cacophony of life's demands into a symphony of balance and tranquillity. Today, become the conductor of your inner orchestra, bringing each element into a harmonious arrangement."

Prayer

Divine Peace, bless me with the wisdom to orchestrate the diverse notes within me. May the melody of my emotions harmonize with the rhythm of my thoughts, creating a symphony of inner Peace and balance. Guide me in crafting a life that resonates with the elegance of inner harmony. Amen.

DAY 186

INNER STRENGTH

Reflection

In the quiet chambers of your soul, take a moment to reflect on the reservoir of strength that resides within. Consider the challenges you've faced and the triumphs you've celebrated. What whispers of resilience and fortitude echo within you, waiting to be acknowledged and embraced?

Inspiration

Inner strength is the silent melody playing in our life background. The quiet force carries us through storms, the unwavering foundation upon which our resilience is built. Today, listen to the song of your inner strength and let it guide you with grace and resilience.

Prayer

Gentle Guardian, guide me in embracing challenges as opportunities to reveal the extraordinary depth of my inner fortitude. As I navigate the complexities of life, may I draw from the wellspring of strength within me. Amen.

DAY 187

EMPOWERED CHOICES

Reflection

Reflect on the power within you to make choices that align with your true self. How can you empower yourself through intentional and authentic decisions?

Inspiration

Empowerment is a gift you give yourself with every choice. Choose with intention and watch as your life becomes a canvas of empowered living and limitless possibilities.

Prayer

Empowering Spirit, guide me in making choices that align with my authentic self. May each decision be a step toward a life of empowerment and purpose. Amen.

DAY 188

COURAGEOUS CHOICES

Reflection

Reflect on the choices before you. How can courage be the guiding force in your decision-making today?

Inspiration

In the tapestry of life, every thread is a choice. Let courage be the vibrant hue that adds depth and richness to the unfolding masterpiece of your journey.

Prayer

Courageous Creator, infuse my choices with the boldness to embrace growth and possibility. May my decisions reflect the strength within me. Amen.

DAY 189

FORGIVENESS FREES

Reflection

Reflect on the weight lifted when forgiveness is offered and received. Today, release any lingering resentment, allowing the freedom of forgiveness to blossom.

Inspiration

Forgiveness unlocks the chains of the past. As you turn the key, feel the door swing open to a future bathed in the light of boundless possibilities.

Prayer

Divine Source, grant me the strength to forgive and the wisdom to release the shackles of resentment. May my heart be a sanctuary of compassion and freedom.
Amen.

DAY 190

GRACEFUL GROWTH

Reflection

Contemplate how challenges have been catalysts for your growth. Now, think of any challenge or obstacle you face and find an opportunity for graceful expansion.

Inspiration

In the garden of life, challenges are the nutrients for graceful growth. Embrace them and watch yourself bloom into the extraordinary being you are meant to be.

Prayer

Sovereign God, guide me through the seasons of change with grace. May my roots be strong, my branches reach high, and my heart open to growth's beauty. Amen.

DAY 191

GRATITUDE JOURNALING

Reflection

Explore the pages of your gratitude journal. With each entry, feel the warmth of appreciation fill your being. Today, acknowledge the abundance that surrounds you.

Inspiration

In the art of living, gratitude is the brush that paints every moment with vibrant hues of joy. Dip your brush often and create a masterpiece of a grateful heart.

Prayer

Creator of Joy, I express my gratitude for the tapestry of blessings woven into my life. May my heart be a canvas painted with the colours of appreciation. Amen.

DAY 192

ACTS OF KINDNESS

Reflection

Consider the impact of small acts of kindness. Today, purposefully spread positivity like petals, leaving a trail of beauty in your wake.

Inspiration

Kindness is the language of the heart. Speak it fluently and watch as the world transforms into a garden of compassion, one act of kindness at a time.

Prayer

Architect of Compassion, inspire me to build bridges of kindness. May my actions create a legacy of love that transcends time and space. Amen.

DAY 193

SERENE DAY

Reflection

As the week unfolds, find serenity in the stillness of this day. Allow the calm to rejuvenate your Spirit and prepare you for the extraordinary days ahead. Set aside a Day for self-care.

Inspiration

In the symphony of life, let this Day be a restful note, a pause that allows the melody of serenity to linger and harmonise with the rhythm of your soul.

Prayer

Eternal Peace, grant me a serenity today. Let toDay be a Day of rest and rejuvenation. May my Spirit be refreshed and my heart be ready for the beauty of the coming week. Amen.

DAY 194

MINDFUL LIVING

Reflection

Mindful living is the practice of being fully present in each moment. Reflect on the beauty found in mindfulness. How can you cultivate a deeper awareness of the beauty that unfolds in every breath and step of your journey?

Inspiration

Mindful living is the art of savouring the exquisite details of existence. Today, immerse yourself in the present moment and let the beauty of mindful living be a balm for your soul.

Prayer

Guiding Spirit, grant me the grace to live fully in each moment. May the beauty of mindful living infuse my days with tranquillity, gratitude, and a deep appreciation for the richness of life. Amen.

DAY 195

POSITIVITY BOOST

Reflection

Take a moment to reflect on the power of positivity. How does a positive mindset influence your thoughts, actions, and well-being?

Inspiration

Positivity is the spark that ignites the flame of extraordinary living. Let it be the guiding light that brightens your path and transforms challenges into opportunities.

Prayer

Giver of Light, infuse my Spirit with the radiance of positivity. May my days be adorned with the brilliance of optimism and joy. Amen.

DAY 196

POSITIVE AFFIRMATIONS

Reflection

Consider the impact of the words you speak to yourself. How can positive affirmations shape your self-perception and empower your journey?

Inspiration

With each affirmation, you craft the narrative of your life. Speak words of empowerment, and watch as the story unfolds with beauty, strength, and unwavering positivity.

Prayer

Divine Wisdom, guide me to speak affirmations that resonate with the melody of my soul and shape my destiny. May my self-talk be a symphony of positivity. Amen.

DAY 197

RADIANT RELATIONSHIPS

Reflection

Reflect on the relationships that bring radiance to your life. Think of three or four ways to nurture and celebrate these connections today.

Inspiration

In the garden of relationships, let love be the sunlight that nurtures and the water that sustains. Cultivate radiant connections that blossom with shared joy and positivity."

Prayer

Eternal One, bless my relationships with the glow of radiance. May love and positivity flourish in the fertile soil of our shared experiences. Amen.

DAY 198

HARMONY IN RELATIONSHIPS

Reflection

Contemplate the balance required for harmonious relationships. How can you contribute to the symphony of your connection and understanding?

Inspiration

Harmony in relationships is the sweet melody that resonates in the heart. Tune into the frequencies of empathy, communication, and love, creating a masterpiece of interconnected souls.

Prayer

Divine Harmony, orchestrate my relationships with the sweet notes of understanding and compassion. May the music of connection be harmonious and enduring. Amen.

DAY 199

JOYFUL JOURNALING

Reflection

Explore the joy found in the act of journaling. What moments of gratitude and positivity can you capture on the pages of your journal today?

Inspiration

Journaling is the art of capturing joy in words. With each pen stroke, you paint a canvas of gratitude, turning ordinary moments into extraordinary memories.

Prayer

Creator of Memories, guide my pen as I journal the symphony of joy in my life. May my words be a testament to the beauty that surrounds me. Amen.

DAY 200

LAUGH OUT LOUD

Reflection

Take a moment to reflect on the healing power of laughter. When was the last time you laughed wholeheartedly, embracing the joy that it brings?

Inspiration

Laughter is the melody of a joyful heart. Let it resonate in the chambers of your soul, bringing lightness and a sense of liberation to your being.

Prayer

Joyful Creator, bless me with the gift of laughter. May the echoes of mirth fill my days with light and levity. May I always find a reason to laugh out loud. Amen.

DAY 201

DO IT WITH FEAR

Reflection

Contemplate the areas in your life where Fear may be holding you back. How can you approach toDay with a fearless spirit, embracing challenges as opportunities for growth?

Inspiration

On this Fearless day, let courage be your compass. Navigate the Day boldly, knowing that every step taken in the face of Fear is a triumph of the spirit.

Prayer

Courageous Guide, grant me the courage to face challenges head-on. May my actions toDay be fuelled by bravery and a loving heart. Amen.

DAY 202

SELF-LOVE TREAT

Reflection

Reflect on the importance of self-love. How can you practice kindness and acceptance towards yourself today?

Inspiration

Self-love is the foundation of extraordinary living. Make this your Self-Love day, shower yourself with the same compassion and care you so willingly give to others.

Prayer

Compassionate Source, fill my heart with Love for myself. May I embrace my flaws and celebrate the uniqueness that makes me who I am. Amen.

DAY 203

STRENGTH IN COMMUNITY

Reflection

Reflect on the connections that make up your community. Who are they, and how can you contribute to the strength and support within your circle?

Inspiration

Each thread that holds a community tells a story, and together, they create a fabric of strength. Strengthen the bonds that tie you to others and find empowerment in unity.

Prayer

Divine Love, bless my community with strength. May our connections be a source of support and resilience. Amen.

DAY 204

STRENGTH IN VULNERABILITY

Reflection

Consider the beauty and strength found in vulnerability. How can you open yourself to authenticity and connect with others deeper?

Inspiration

Vulnerability is the gateway to profound connection and inner strength. Embrace the courage to be authentic, allowing your true self to shine gracefully.

Prayer

Tender Creator, grant me the strength found in vulnerability. May I embrace authenticity, connecting with others with an open heart. Amen.

DAY 205

MIND-BODY BALANCE

Reflection

Reflect on the interconnectedness of your mind and body. How can you cultivate balance and harmony between the two for a more holistic well-being?

Inspiration

In the dance of life, find harmony in the union of mind and body. Today, prioritise practices that nourish both, creating a symphony of balance that resonates throughout your being.

Prayer

Harmonious Creator, guide me in achieving a balance between mind and body. May my actions and thoughts align, creating a serene and balanced existence. Amen.

DAY 206

BALANCED LIVING

Reflection

Consider the balance in your life. Where can you harmonise work, play, rest, and activity to create a more balanced and fulfilling existence?

Inspiration

Balance is the art of orchestrating life's elements into a symphony of well-being. Strive for equilibrium and watch as the music of balance transforms your days.

Prayer

Divine Guide, lead me in creating a life of balance. May I gracefully navigate the ebb and flow, finding serenity in the equilibrium of my journey. Amen.

DAY 207

RADIANT REFLECTION

Reflection

Look in the mirror and truly see yourself. What inner radiance can you acknowledge and celebrate today?

Inspiration

Reflection is the mirror of the soul. See the radiance within; you are a masterpiece, a reflection of divine artistry, and your light is meant to shine.

Prayer

Creator of Radiance, let the light within me shine brightly. May my reflection reveal the beauty of my soul. Amen.

DAY 208

MINDFUL MOVEMENT

Reflection

As you move through the day, practice mindfulness in every step. How can you infuse intention into your actions, savouring each moment?

Inspiration

In the dance of life, move with purpose and mindfulness. Each step, each breath, is a chance to be present, to savour the exquisite beauty of the present moment.

Prayer

Guiding Presence, bless my movements with mindfulness. May I dance through life with intention and graceful steps, knowing you are always with me. Amen.

DAY 209

MIND-BODY CONNECTION

Reflection

Reflect on the profound connection between your mind and body. How can you nurture this symbiotic relationship for overall well-being?

Inspiration

Your body is a canvas, and your mind is the artist. Nurture the connection between the two, painting a masterpiece of holistic well-being and harmony.

Prayer

Dear Sculptor of Wellness, guide me in honouring the sacred bond between mind and body. May I care for both with grace, love and intention. Amen.

DAY 210

POSITIVE IMPACT

Reflection

Consider the impact you have on others. Today, think of ways your words and actions can positively affect the lives of those around you.

Inspiration

In the grand tapestry of humanity, your impact is a thread that weaves through the lives of others. Choose to leave a legacy of positivity, kindness, and love.

Prayer

Source of Light, empower me to be a force for positive impact. May my actions echo with kindness, uplifting those in my orbit. Amen.

DAY 211

THE EXTRAORDINARY JOURNEY

Reflection

Reflect on the extraordinary journey you've undertaken. What lessons have you learned, and how have you grown?

Inspiration

The extraordinary journey is not about the destination but the lessons learned, the growth experienced, and the love shared. Celebrate the beauty of your unique path.

Prayer

Divine Guide, thank you for the extraordinary journey of my life. May I walk with grace, wisdom, and an open heart, embracing the adventures ahead.

DAY 212

GRATEFUL ENDINGS

Reflection

As the sun sets on another chapter of your life, take a moment to reflect on the journey that brought you to this point. Consider the lessons, the joys, and the growth that have graced your path. What blessings have adorned your days, and how can gratitude illuminate the way forward?

Inspiration

Grateful endings are the punctuation marks that punctuate the chapters of our lives. Each closure is an opportunity for reflection, for recognising the beauty that unfolded, and for expressing gratitude for the richness of the journey. Today, embrace the art of grateful endings and let them pave the way for new beginnings.

Prayer

Eternal One, as I bid farewell to this chapter, fill my heart with gratitude for the moments that have shaped me. May I gracefully release what no longer serves, and may gratitude be the compass guiding me into the next exquisite chapter of my extraordinary journey. Amen.

INSPIRATION

DAY 213

DREAM-WEAVING

Reflection

Like a skilled weaver, your aspirations and passions interlace to create the fabric of your life.

Today, pause and consider the threads of your dreams. What vivid hues do you wish to intertwine to create the masterpiece of your extraordinary life?

Inspiration

"Every dream begins with a dreamer. Always remember, you have within you the strength, the patience, and the passion to reach for the stars and change the world." - Harriet Tubman.

Prayer

Graceful Creator, guide my hands as I weave the dreams of my heart. May each thread be a testament to the extraordinary life you envision for me. Amen.

DAY 214

CREATIVE SPARKS

Reflection

Creativity is the spark that ignites the extraordinary. Today, recognise the sparks of creativity within you and reflect on how your unique creativity can illuminate the world around you.

Inspiration

"Creativity is intelligence having fun."
- Albert Einstein.

Prayer

Divine Muse, bless me with the sparks of creativity. May my thoughts blaze with inspiration, my ideas dance with grace, and my imagination flow like a river of endless inspiration. Amen.

DAY 215

WANDERLUST DAY

Reflection

The world is a vast tapestry waiting to be explored. Whether in your thoughts or physical journey, allow curiosity to guide you. Today, embrace the Spirit of wanderlust and open your heart to the beauty of the unknown.

Inspiration

Wanderlust is the soul's compass, guiding us to discover the extraordinary in every corner of existence. Let curiosity be your passport to a life well explored.

Prayer

Divine Guide, lead me to uncharted realms. As I step into the world, may I find extraordinary moments in every corner. Bless my travels with safety, wonder, and an open heart. Amen.

DAY 216

VISIONARY ARTISTRY

Reflection

Art is the language of the soul. You are the artist of your life, painting strokes of purpose and meaning. Today, focus on the canvas of your aspirations. What masterpiece does your heart yearn to create?

Inspiration

"The artist is not a special kind of person; rather, each person is a special kind of artist." - Ananda Coomaraswamy.

Prayer

Artistic Creator, grant me the wisdom to paint with purpose and the grace to infuse my life with the hues of joy and fulfilment. Let my life be painted with love, happiness, and purpose. Amen.

DAY 217

IMAGINATIVE PLAY

Reflection

Imagination is the playground of the soul. Immerse yourself in the whimsical realms of imagination. Today, release your inner child and let the laughter of your Spirit echo through the corridors of your heart. How can you infuse your Day with the spontaneity and joy of imaginative play?

Inspiration

In the dance of life, playfulness is the rhythm. Let the music of your imagination guide your steps, and embrace the extraordinary joy found in the simplicity of play.

Prayer

Playful Spirit, bless me with the freedom to embrace the whimsy of imagination. May my days be adorned with the dance of imagination, and may my heart find joy in the simple act of play. Amen.

DAY 218

FANTASY VOYAGE

Reflection

Embark on a fantasy voyage within your mind. Let your thoughts sail into the uncharted seas of your imagination. What fantastical landscapes can your mind explore today?

Inspiration

The mind is a vessel, and fantasy is its wind. Let your thoughts set sail on the voyage of imagination, exploring the extraordinary realms of your dreams.

Prayer

Divine Guide, guide my thoughts on this fantasy voyage. May the winds of imagination carry me to extraordinary destinations where possibilities are as vast as the starry skies, unveiling the magic within. Amen."

DAY 219

PERSONAL MANIFESTO

Reflection

Craft a manifesto that echoes the essence of your being. What principles and aspirations will you declare to the world and to yourself? Reflect on the power of a personal manifesto to guide your journey.

Inspiration

"A personal manifesto is a declaration of your core values and beliefs, as well as your vision for your life." - Gabrielle Bernstein.

Prayer

Author of My Destiny, as I pen my personal manifesto, may my words be a beacon guiding me toward a life filled with purpose, authenticity, and extraordinary living. Amen.

DAY 220

DREAM DIALOGUE

Reflection

In the quiet moments between wakefulness and slumber, our dreams whisper secrets of our deepest desires. Today, engage in a dialogue with your dreams. What truths do they reveal about the life you long for?

Inspiration

Your dreams are a reflection of your soul's desires. Listen carefully, for within them lies the roadmap to your extraordinary journey.

Prayer

Gentle Dreamweaver, unveil the visions of my soul as I engage in this dialogue. Illuminate the path to an extraordinary life through the language of my dreams. May my dreams guide me toward the incredible life I am meant to live. Amen.

DAY 221

DIGITAL DETOX DAY

Reflection

In a world buzzing with constant connectivity, silence speaks volumes. ToDay is a sanctuary of solitude, so reflect on the impact of digital detox on your mental and spiritual well-being.

Inspiration

In the hush of digital silence, rediscover the beauty of genuine connection—with yourself, others, and the world.

Prayer

Author of Peace, grant me the strength to detach from the digital cacophony. As I unplug from the digital noise, fill the spaces with the serenity of your presence. Grant me clarity and peace during this detox day.

DAY 222

NATURE RETREAT

Reflection

Nature is a sanctuary for the soul. Today, retreat to its soothing embrace. What whispers of wisdom does the natural world have for you?

Inspiration

Amidst the rustling leaves and dancing streams, discover the extraordinary serenity nature graciously offers to all seeking.

Prayer

Dear Universe, as I retreat into your sacred spaces, envelop me in the tranquillity of your beauty. May my soul find solace and restoration in your embrace. Amen.

DAY 223

PAMPER YOURSELF

Reflection
Self-care is an art that adorns the canvas of our well-being. Today, indulge in acts of kindness towards yourself. What lavish moments of self-care will you gift to your soul?

Inspiration
"Nourishing yourself in a way that helps you blossom in the direction you want to go is attainable, and you are worth the effort." - Deborah Day.

Prayer
Divine Love, as I lavish care upon my being, let the grace of your Love infuse every moment. May each act be a ritual of Love and celebration of my worthiness. Let self-compassion blossom into an extraordinary garden of well-being. Amen.

DAY 224

SLEEP SANCTUARY

Reflection

Dreams unfold in the embrace of restful sleep, and the spirit rejuvenates. Reflect on the sanctuary your sleep provides and how it contributes to an extraordinary life. How can you transform your sleep into a refuge for exceptional renewal?

Inspiration

"Sleep is the best meditation." - Dalai Lama

Prayer

Guardian of Dreams, as I enter the sleep sanctuary, wrap me in the comfort of peace. May each dream be a step towards an extraordinary awakening and each slumber a gateway to boundless potential. Amen.

DAY 225

GRATITUDE JOURNALING

Reflection

Gratitude is the language of the heart. Reflect on the moments that stir gratitude within you. What jewels of gratitude can you discover in the tapestry of your day?

Inspiration

In the art of gratitude, every stroke of appreciation adds brilliance to the canvas of your extraordinary life.

Prayer

Custodian of Gratitude, grant me the wisdom to see the extraordinary in the ordinary. May gratitude be the melody that orchestrates my life, and may my gratitude journal become a masterpiece of joy and abundance. Amen.

DAY 226

GRATITUDE GARDEN

Reflection

In the garden of your heart, cultivate the flowers of gratitude. Reflect on the beauty surrounding you and the moments blooming into blessings. What seeds of gratitude can you sow today?

Inspiration

"Gratitude turns what we have into enough."
– Aesop.

Prayer

Cultivator of Joy, as I tend to the garden of gratitude within, may my heart bloom with appreciation for the extraordinary gifts life bestows upon me. Amen.

DAY 227

MINDFULNESS MEDITATION

Reflection

In the stillness of this moment, immerse yourself in mindfulness. What revelations does the present hold when gently directing your awareness to the now? Reflect on the peace found in mindful presence. How can mindful awareness enrich the canvas of your life?

Inspiration

"The present moment is filled with joy and happiness. If you are attentive, you will see it." - Thich Nhat Hanh.

Prayer

Divine presence, as I engage in mindfulness meditation, may my spirit be illuminated by the tranquillity found in the sacred simplicity of each passing moment. Amen.

DAY 228

YOGA HARMONY

Reflection

Harmony is the dance of body and soul. Reflect on the harmony that emerges when mind, body, and spirit unite on the mat. How can you cultivate balance and serenity within as you flow through the movements of yoga? How can the rhythm of yoga guide you toward extraordinary living?

Inspiration

Yoga is the journey of the self, through the self, to the self." - The Bhagavad Gita.

Prayer

Architect of Harmony, as I engage in the graceful dance of yoga, may my spirit find balance and my body resonate with the rhythm of divine energy. Amen.

DAY 229

LETTING GO RITUAL

Reflection

Reflect on the art of letting go and the freedom it brings. Release the burdens that weigh upon your spirit. What anchors can you release to allow your soul to soar? Reflect on the liberation found in surrendering that which no longer serves your extraordinary journey.

Inspiration

"Letting go gives us freedom, and freedom is the only condition for happiness."
- Thich Nhat Hanh.

Prayer

Divine Peace, as I engage in the letting go ritual, may my spirit be unburdened and soar with newfound lightness. Amen.

DAY 230

SILENT REFLECTION

Reflection

Silence is the canvas upon which profound insights are painted. Reflect on the power of stillness; what truths can you uncover about yourself and the world? What whispers of wisdom does silence bring?

Inspiration

"In the attitude of silence, the soul finds the path in a clearer light." - Mahatma Gandhi.

Prayer

Guardian of my Soul, as I enter the hallowed space of quiet reflection, may the whispers of my soul be heard and the extraordinary truths of my being revealed. Amen.

DAY 231

LOVING-KINDNESS MEDITATION

Reflection

Love is the essence of the extraordinary. Who in your life, including yourself, could benefit from the warmth of loving-kindness? How can the gentle embrace of compassion radiate outward, creating ripples of the extraordinary?

Inspiration

"May all beings be happy, may all beings be healthy, may all beings be safe, may all beings be at ease." - Traditional Metta Prayer

Prayer

Architect of Compassion, as I engage in loving-kindness meditation, may my heart be a sanctuary of love and radiate with love, and my spirit becomes a vessel of extraordinary kindness. Amen.

DAY 232

HARMONY IN ROUTINE

Reflection

In the pulse of your daily routine, seek the melody of harmony. What harmonies can be found in the rhythm of your everyDay life? Reflect on the artistry of infusing each routine with purpose and grace. How can the symphony of your habits and tasks create a life that resonates with tranquillity?

Inspiration

"Ordinary life does not interest me. I seek only the high moments." - Anais Nin.

Prayer

Source of Life, may my routine be a harmonious composition, weaving moments of joy and Peace into the tapestry of my extraordinary life. Amen.

DAY 233

BREATH OF CALM

Reflection

The breath is the conductor of calm. Discover the calming rhythm of life within the rise and fall of each breath. Reflect on the power of intentional breathing to bring calm to even the busiest moments.

Inspiration

With each breath, embrace the calm within, a sanctuary amid life's bustling symphony.

Prayer

Breath of Life, infuse my being with the calm of each intentional inhale. May my breath be a source of tranquillity amid life's storms.
Amen.

DAY 234

SOULFUL SILENCE

Reflection

In the sanctuary of silence, the soul finds its voice. What whispers of wisdom can be heard when you quiet the noise around and within you? Reflect on the depth and beauty found in soulful silence.

Inspiration

"True silence is the rest of the mind and is to the spirit what sleep is to the body, nourishment and refreshment." - William Penn.

Prayer

Divine Presence, may the silence within me be a sanctuary where my soul rests and my spirit is rejuvenated. Amen.

DAY 235

REFLECTION AND INTEGRATION

Reflection

Reflection is the mirror through which growth is witnessed. How can the lessons of the past integrate seamlessly into the present? Reflect on the art of learning from experience. Reflect on the beauty of evolving through thoughtful contemplation.

Inspiration

"Your visions will become clear only when you look into your heart. Who looks outside, dreams, looks inside, awakes." - Carl Jung.

Prayer

Seer of Souls, as I reflect on my path, may the wisdom gained become an integral part of my being, guiding me toward extraordinary living. Amen.

DAY 236

ACTIONABLE GOALS

Reflection

Dreams become extraordinary when fuelled by actionable goals. What steps can you take toDay to breathe life into your aspirations? Reflect on the power of deliberate actions in shaping the extraordinary life you desire.

Inspiration

"Setting goals is the first step in turning the invisible into the visible." - Tony Robbins.

Prayer

Architect of Aspirations, may my goals be clear, my path illuminated, and my actions purposeful and may each step be a stride toward an extraordinary destiny. Amen.

DAY 237

COMMUNITY CONNECTION

Reflection

Reflect on the richness of sharing, supporting, and connecting with others.

How can you strengthen the threads that bind you to your community? How can your Presence and engagement enrich the lives of those around you?

Inspiration

"The best way to find yourself is to lose yourself in the service of others." - Mahatma Gandhi.

Prayer

Nurturer of Connections, as I engage with my community, may the bonds of our friendship grow strong, and may our collective spirit be a force that propels us all towards extraordinary living. Amen.

DAY 238

CELEBRATION OF ACHIEVEMENTS

Reflection

Pause and revel in the glow of your achievements. What milestones, big or small, have shaped your extraordinary journey? Reflect on the joy found in acknowledging your accomplishments.

Inspiration

"Celebrate what you've accomplished but raise the bar a little higher each time you succeed." - Mia Hamm.

Prayer

Gifts Giver, as I celebrate my achievements, may gratitude fill my heart, and may the joy of accomplishment pave the way for more extraordinary feats. Amen.

DAY 239

COMMITMENT TO SELF

Reflection

In the quiet chambers of your heart, renew your commitment to yourself. What promises can you make to honour and uplift your own spirit? Reflect on the profound impact of a sincere commitment to self-love.

Inspiration

"Commitment to oneself is the foundation of personal and professional success."
- Vishwas Chavan.

Prayer

Sovereign Spirit, as I recommit to my well-being and growth, may my journey be guided by the light of self-love and unwavering dedication. Amen.

DAY 240

REFLECTIVE JOURNALING

Reflection

The pages of your journal are a canvas for your thoughts and dreams. What reflections will you paint today? Reflect on capturing your innermost thoughts in the strokes of written expression.

Inspiration

"Journal writing, when it becomes a ritual for transformation, is not only life-changing but life-expanding." - Jen Williamson.

Prayer

Wordsmith of the Soul, as I journal my reflections, may the pages be a canvas for the expression of my soul, and may my self-discovery be a journey filled with grace.
Amen.

DAY 241

EMPOWERMENT AFFIRMATIONS

Reflection

Speak words of empowerment into the universe. What affirmations can you declare to uplift and strengthen your spirit? Reflect on the transformative power of positive self-talk.

Inspiration

"Your affirmations have to be in the present tense. Be positive and state your affirmation in the most positive way you can." - Louise Hay

Prayer

Ever Present One, may my words echo with confidence, resilience, and unwavering belief in my ability to create an extraordinary life. May the affirmations I declare be a melody that resonates with the strength and courage within my being. Amen.

DAY 242

COMPASSION CULTIVATION

Reflection

Cultivate the garden of your heart with seeds of compassion. How can you extend kindness, both to yourself and others, today? Reflect on the gentle power of empathy to transform lives.

Inspiration

"Compassion brings us to a stop, and for a moment, we rise above ourselves."
- Mason Cooley.

Prayer

Compassionate One, may my heart be a garden where the flowers of kindness bloom, nourished by the waters of empathy and understanding and may compassion ripple through my interactions. Amen.

DAY 243

JOYFUL MOVEMENT

Reflection

In the rhythm of movement, find the joy that dances within you. How can you infuse your Day with activities that bring lightness to your spirit? Reflect on the liberation found in the celebration of your body's grace.

Inspiration

"Movement is a medicine for creating change in a person's physical, emotional, and mental states." - Carol Welch.

Prayer

Choreographer of Joy, as I move with grace and freedom, may my spirit revel in the joy in life's dance. Amen.

DAY 244

EMBRACING A NEW DAY WITH GRACE

Reflection

As the sun rises, we are granted a new beginning. Reflect on the Grace that comes with each dawn, wiping away yesterday's mistakes and offering a canvas for a fresh start.

Inspiration

With each sunrise, we are given a chance to rewrite our story with Grace. Embrace the dawn, and let its light guide your steps today.

Prayer

Dear Universe, may grace accompany me as I step into this new day. May my actions be guided by kindness, my words be wrapped in elegance, and my heart open to the beauty surrounding me. Amen.

DAY 245

REFLECTING ON THE GRACE OF FORGIVENESS, BOTH RECEIVING AND EXTENDING IT

Reflection

Consider the weight lifted when you forgive and the freedom of receiving forgiveness today. Reflect on the Grace bestowed upon us through this powerful act.

Inspiration

In forgiveness, we find a grace that heals both the giver and the receiver. Let go of resentment, and you make space for love to flourish.

Prayer

Dear Source of Grace, grant me the strength to forgive others as I seek forgiveness myself. May my heart be lightened by the elegance of forgiveness, and may I extend it generously to others. Amen.

DAY 246

GRACE IN ADVERSITY

Reflection
Amid challenges, Grace is a beacon of hope. Reflect on past adversities and the strength that arose, recognising the Grace that carried you through.

Inspiration
Adversity is not the end but a new beginning. In the face of challenges, we discover the Grace that transforms difficulties into stepping stones.

Prayer
Divine Grace, as I face challenges, may I find strength and resilience. Cloak me in the elegance of Grace, that I may navigate storms with poise and emerge stronger on the other side. Amen.

DAY 247

RADICAL ACCEPTANCE

Reflection

True Grace begins with acceptance. Reflect on the beauty that unfolds when we accept ourselves and others without judgment, allowing love to blossom.

Inspiration

We must start by accepting ourselves and others with radical love to fully embrace Grace. In this acceptance, we discover the stylish art of living authentically.

Prayer

Dear Creator of Grace, teach me the art of radical acceptance. May I embrace myself and others with love and understanding, celebrating the unique beauty each of us brings to the world. Amen.

DAY 248

GRACEFUL ACTS OF KINDNESS

Reflection

Today, ponder the ripple effect of graceful acts of kindness. Reflect on the joy that comes from positively impacting others, infusing your actions with style and Grace.

Inspiration

Kindness is the language of Grace. As you go about your day, let your actions be a stylish symphony of kindness, leaving a trail of warmth wherever you go.

Prayer

Dear Giver of Grace, empower me to be a vessel of kindness today. May my deeds be as elegant as a well-tailored suit, leaving an indelible mark of Grace on the hearts of those I encounter. Amen.

DAY 249

STRENGTH THROUGH VULNERABILITY

Reflection

In vulnerability, we find strength. Reflect on the power of embracing your authentic self, acknowledging that true strength is found in authenticity.

Inspiration

Authenticity is the epitome of strength. Today, embrace your vulnerabilities as badges of honour, weaving them into the tapestry of your unique and powerful self.

Prayer

Dear God, guide me to embrace my true self. May I find strength in vulnerability and wear my authenticity with Grace and confidence. Amen.

DAY 250

COMMITMENT TO GROWTH

Reflection

Growth is a lifelong journey. Reflect on the importance of committing to continuous learning and evolution, understanding that each experience is a stepping stone toward extraordinary living. How are you demonstrating your commitment to continuously evolving and learning?

Inspiration

A commitment to growth is a commitment to a life well-lived. Today, embrace the journey of continuous learning, for you'll find the seeds of an extraordinary existence.

Prayer

Eternal Teacher, illuminate my path of learning. May I approach each Day with a commitment to evolve, and may pursuing knowledge be my stylish companion on this journey. Amen.

DAY 251

CULTIVATING LOVE AND UNDERSTANDING

Reflection

Reflect on the relationships in your life and the Grace that comes from cultivating love and understanding. Consider how the Grace of connection enriches the fabric of your existence.

Inspiration

In the dance of relationships, Grace is the music. Cultivate love and understanding in your connections, and you'll find that every step becomes a stylish expression of the heart.

Prayer

Forever Friend, guide me in the dance of love and understanding. May my relationships be a stylish symphony of Grace, enriching my life and the lives of those around me. Amen.

DAY 252

BUILDING A SUPPORTIVE COMMUNITY

Reflection

Today, reflect on the strength that comes from unity. Consider the power of a supportive community, recognising that we can achieve extraordinary feats together.

Inspiration

In unity, strength becomes an unstoppable force. Today, celebrate the bonds that connect us and recognise the stylish beauty that arises when we stand together.

Prayer

Spirit of Unity, bless the bonds of community around me. May our collective strength be a testament to the elegance that arises when we support and uplift one another. Amen.

DAY 253

DEDICATION TO PURPOSE

Reflection

Reflect on the significance of living with purpose. Consider how dedication to a purpose-driven life infuses each Day with meaning and style.

Inspiration

A purpose-driven life is a life of significance. Today, reflect on your purpose and commit to living with dedication, for you'll discover the true essence of extraordinary living.

Prayer

Dear Guiding Light of Purpose, illuminate my path with clarity. May my actions be purposeful, my pursuits be meaningful, and my journey is a stylish testament to a life well-committed. Amen.

DAY 254

FAITHFUL COMMITMENT

Reflection
Today, reflect on the beauty of commitment in your relationships, friendships, and partnerships. Consider the strength and grace from faithful commitment to those you hold dear.

Inspiration
In the tapestry of life, commitment is the golden thread that weaves bonds of love and trust. Today, celebrate the richness that faithful commitment brings to your relationships.

Prayer
Dear Lord, grace my relationships with loyalty and devotion. May my commitments be as timeless and elegant as a classic piece of art, adding beauty to the canvas of my life. Amen.

DAY 255

DISCIPLINE, PERSONAL AND SPIRITUAL GROWTH

Reflection

Reflect on the role of discipline in fostering commitment, personal development and spiritual growth. Consider the grace that comes from a disciplined, focused life.

Inspiration

Discipline bridges goals and accomplishments. Today, embrace the stylish art of self-discipline, knowing it is the key to unlocking extraordinary living.

Prayer

Gracious God, guide me in the dance of commitment and self-discipline. May my journey be marked by the elegance of intentional living and the grace of focused purpose. Amen.

DAY 256

SACRIFICE AND FULFILLING LONG-TERM COMMITMENTS

Reflection

Today, ponder the concept of sacrifice in the context of long-term commitments. Reflect on the grace that comes from giving up something toDay for the promise of a better tomorrow.

Inspiration

Sacrifice is the currency of commitment. Today, recognise the stylish beauty that arises from selfless acts, knowing that every sacrifice sows seeds for a future of abundance.

Prayer

Gracious God, grant me the strength to give generously for my commitments. May my sacrifices be made with grace and purpose, adding a touch of elegance to my journey. Amen.

DAY 257

INTEGRITY IN ALL ASPECTS OF LIFE

Reflection

Reflect on the importance of integrity and honouring your commitments to yourself and others. Consider the grace that arises from a life aligned with truth and authenticity.

Inspiration

Integrity is the cornerstone of commitment. Today, commit to walking the path of honesty and authenticity; in it, you'll find the stylish strength that comes from living with integrity.

Prayer

Dear Guardian, guide my commitment to live with truth and honour. May my actions reflect my values, and may the elegance of integrity be my constant companion. Amen.

DAY 258

STRENGTH IN SURRENDER

Reflection

Today, reflect on the paradoxical strength found in surrender. Consider the grace that arises when you release control and trust in the greater flow of life.

Inspiration

Strength is not always in control but in surrender. Today, find power in letting go, allowing the river of life to carry you with grace and ease.

Prayer

Dear Source of Life, teach me the art of surrender. May I release my grip on outcomes and trust in the elegant dance of destiny. Grant me the strength to find power in letting go. Amen.

DAY 259

LIVING IN THE PRESENT MOMENT

Reflection

Reflect on the commitment to mindfulness and living in the present moment. Consider the grace that comes from fully immersing yourself in the beauty of now.

Inspiration

In the stillness of the present moment, grace unfolds. Today, commit to mindfulness, savouring each breath's elegance and the now's stylish beauty.

Prayer

Dear Keeper of Time, anchor me in the present. May my commitment to mindfulness be a source of grace, allowing me to appreciate the beauty that unfolds in every fleeting moment. Amen.

DAY 260

INSPIRING OTHERS WITH GRACEFUL ACTIONS

Reflection

Today, reflect on the concept of graceful leadership. Consider the impact of leading gracefully inspiring others through your actions and commitment.

Inspiration

True leaders inspire with grace. Today, commit to leading with elegance, knowing that your actions have the power to uplift and empower those around you.

Prayer

Master of the Universe, guide me in the commitment to lead with wisdom and compassion. May my actions inspire others to reach new heights, and may my leadership be a stylish beacon of grace. Amen.

DAY 261

TRUSTING THE JOURNEY AND THE PROCESS

Reflection

Today, reflect on the strength that comes from patience. Consider the beauty of trusting the journey, knowing that each step is a part of the graceful process of becoming.

Inspiration

Patience is the art of trusting the process. Today, find strength in the waiting, knowing that each moment is a step toward the extraordinary life you are destined to live.

Prayer

Dear All-Knowing, grant me the strength to be patient. May I trust the journey, understanding that every step, no matter how small, is a graceful part of the more extraordinary tapestry of my life. Amen.

DAY 262

BALANCING GRACE AND STRENGTH

Reflection

Reflect on the delicate dance between grace and strength in your daily life. Consider how finding harmony between these qualities can bring elegance to your every action.

Inspiration

In the dance of life, balance is the key. Today, strive for harmony between grace and strength, knowing that a balanced approach brings forth a life of enduring style.

Prayer

Dear Life Atelier, guide me in balancing grace and strength. May my actions be a stylish expression of this harmonious dance, creating a life of enduring elegance. Amen.

DAY 263

COMMITMENT TO SELF-CARE

Reflection

Reflect on the commitment to self-care and its impact on your well-being. Consider how prioritising self-care contributes to a life of grace and strength.

Inspiration

Self-care is not an indulgence but a commitment to one's well-being. Today, recognise the importance of nurturing yourself, for self-care gives you the grace and strength to face life's challenges.

Prayer

Dear Healer, instil in me a commitment to self-care. May I prioritise my physical, emotional, and spiritual health, and may the grace and strength derived from self-care radiate through my life. Amen.

DAY 264

NAVIGATE ENDINGS WITH GRACE AND STRENGTH

Reflection

Life phases are fun. Looking back and laughing is fun. Today, reflect on the art of graceful endings. Consider how navigating closures with grace and strength brings a sense of completion and style to the chapters of your life.

Inspiration

Endings are not conclusions but transitions. Today, reflect on how to bid farewell with grace, understanding that every ending opens a new, stylish chapter in your journey.

Prayer

Eternal Helper, guide me in the art of graceful endings. May I navigate closures with poise and strength, understanding that each goodbye is a prelude to a new and stylish beginning? Amen.

DAY 265

CELEBRATION OF ACHIEVEMENTS

Reflection

In the symphony of your life, take a moment to applaud the melodies of your achievements. What notes of triumph deserve recognition? Reflect on the beauty found in acknowledging your own victories.

Inspiration

"Celebrate what you've accomplished but raise the bar a little higher each time you succeed." - Mia Hamm.

Prayer

Gracious God, may the applause of my achievements reverberate within, inspiring me to reach new heights on the grand stage of my extraordinary life. Amen.

DAY 266

SPEAKING WITH KINDNESS AND WISDOM

Reflection

Reflect on the power of words. Consider how speaking with kindness and wisdom can infuse grace into your interactions, creating a tapestry of elegance in your relationships.

Inspiration

Words are the brushstrokes of our conversations. Today, choose each word with care, painting a canvas of kindness and wisdom that reflects the stylish masterpiece of your character.

Prayer

Source of all Souls, guide my words with grace. May my speech reflect kindness and wisdom, creating a symphony of elegance in every interaction. Amen.

DAY 267

NAVIGATING CHANGE WITH POISE

Reflection

Today, reflect on the beauty found in transitions. Consider how navigating change with poise allows you to gracefully dance through the chapters of your life.

Inspiration

Life is a series of transitions. Today, embrace the art of navigating change with poise, knowing that you find the seeds of growth and style in every transition.

Prayer

Dear Author of Life, grant me the grace to navigate change with poise. May each transition be a stylish dance, leading me to new and extraordinary heights. Amen.

DAY 268

MINDFUL LIVING

Reflection
Reflect on the art of mindful living. Consider how incorporating grace, strength, and commitment into each moment can transform the ordinary into the extraordinary.

Inspiration
Mindfulness is the key to extraordinary living. Today, infuse grace into your actions, find strength in the present, and commit to fully experiencing the richness of each moment.

Prayer
Eternal Presence, bless me with the grace to live mindfully. May each breath be a reminder of strength and may my commitment to the present moment add an elegant touch to my daily existence. Amen.

DAY 269

DAILY AFFIRMATIONS

Reflection
Reflect on how daily positive affirmations can reinforce grace, strength, and commitment, shaping the narrative of your extraordinary life.

Inspiration
Words spoken to oneself create the script of one's life. Today, craft positive affirmations that reinforce grace, strength, and commitment, paving the way for a stylish and extraordinary journey.

Prayer
Gracious God, inspire my words to shape an extraordinary life. May my affirmations be a stylish declaration of grace, strength, and commitment echoing through the corridors of my soul. Amen.

DAY 270

PRACTICING GRATITUDE TO ENHANCE YOUR LIFE

Reflection

Today, reflect on the transformative power of gratitude. Consider how practising gratitude enhances an extraordinary living experience, adding a touch of style to every moment.

Inspiration

Gratitude is the fragrance of a graceful life. Today, cultivate the art of thankfulness and watch your ordinary moments transform into an extraordinary tapestry of blessings.

Prayer

Dear Giver of Blessings, teach me the art of gratitude. May my heart be a garden of thankfulness, and may the fragrance of grace and abundance infuse every corner of my life. Amen.

DAY 271

SETTING BOUNDARIES

Reflection

Ponder on the benefits of setting healthy boundaries. Consider how this act of strength and grace creates a sanctuary for your well-being and contributes to a stylish and balanced life.

Inspiration

Boundaries are the elegant fences that protect the garden of your soul. Today, explore the strength and grace in setting boundaries, creating a space where you can flourish.

Prayer

Dear Helper, empower me to set and maintain healthy limits. May the boundaries I establish be a stylish fortress, protecting my well-being and allowing me to live with strength and grace. Amen.

DAY 272

BIBLICAL HEROES OF GRACE

Reflection

Reflect on the timeless examples of grace found in the Bible. Consider the stories of biblical heroes whose lives were marked by elegance, kindness, and a profound connection with the divine.

Inspiration

In the pages of the Bible, we find a gallery of grace. Today, draw inspiration from the lives of biblical heroes and let their stories guide you in cultivating a life of enduring elegance.

Prayer

Divine grace, as I navigate my journey, open my heart to receive inspirations from the stories of biblical heroes. May their grace be woven into the fabric of my life, creating a timeless masterpiece. Amen.

DAY 273

STRENGTH IN BIBLICAL NARRATIVES

Reflection

Today, reflect on the narratives of strength and resilience in the Bible. Consider the powerful stories showcasing the unwavering strength of faith and perseverance.

Inspiration

The Bible is a testament to the strength found in faith. Today, explore the narratives of resilience, drawing inspiration from the biblical characters who faced challenges with unyielding strength.

Prayer

Dear Source of Strength, as I face challenges, may the stories of biblical resilience fortify my spirit. Grant me the strength to overcome obstacles with grace and poise, knowing that I can emerge victorious like those before me. Amen.

ABUNDANCE

DAY 274

HARMONY IN CHAOS

Reflection

When anxiety fights to take hold of your heart and chaos tries to consume your atmosphere, invite the Divine to be your peace, for amid life's chaos, there's symphony within. Today, like a conductor orchestrating a masterpiece, seek harmony in discord.

Inspiration

Embrace chaos not as a disturbance but as the canvas for a beautiful composition. Your ability to find balance amid chaos is the melody of extraordinary living.

Prayer

Dear Creator, grant me the wisdom to find serenity amid chaos, the strength to navigate the storms gracefully, and the insight to recognise the beauty in life's unpredictable dance. Amen.

DAY 275

THE ART OF PRIORITISATION

Reflection

Life is a canvas, and prioritisation is the brushstroke that creates a masterpiece. Identify the essential strokes, and watch as the art of your life unfolds with elegance.

Inspiration

Prioritise with the precision of a sculptor carving away the unnecessary, revealing the true beauty beneath. Each prioritised task is a step toward a life of purpose and order.

Prayer

Divine Guide, grant me clarity to discern my priorities, the strength to focus on what truly matters, and the grace to let go of what hinders my journey toward extraordinary living. Amen.

DAY 276

CREATIVE FLOW

Reflection

Allow the river of creativity to flow freely within. Like a gentle stream, creativity can carve new paths and nourish the landscapes of your mind.

Inspiration

Creativity is not a force to be controlled but a current to be ridden. Dive into its flow and let it carry you to destinations unknown, painting your life with vibrant and unforeseen hues.

Prayer

Source of Creativity, bless me with the courage to explore the depths of my imagination, the freedom to express my unique creativity, and the joy that comes from embracing the flow of inspiration. Amen.

DAY 277

STRUCTURED SERENITY

Reflection

A well-ordered life is a canvas awaiting the strokes of tranquillity. Today, in the routine structure, discover the serenity of knowing each moment has its place.

Inspiration

Your life is a work of art, and routine is the frame that enhances its beauty. Within the structure, find freedom, and within order, find serenity.

Prayer

Divine Architect, guide me in constructing a life of purpose and order. May each moment find its place, and may the structure of my days be a testament to the serenity within. Amen.

DAY 278

MINDFUL MORNING RITUALS

Reflection

As the sun rises, so does the opportunity for a new beginning. Start each Day with intention, allowing the morning rituals to be the foundation of a purposeful and mindful existence.

Inspiration

In the quiet moments of the morning, discover the power to set the tone for the day. Mindful morning rituals are the keys that unlock the extraordinary potential within you.

Prayer

Morning Light, infuse my rituals with mindfulness. May each action be a step towards purpose, each moment a reminder of the gift of a new day, and each breath an affirmation of life's beauty. Amen.

DAY 279

INNOVATE YOUR DAY

Reflection

ToDay is a canvas awaiting your creative brush. Innovate your Day with the spirit of an artist, infusing even the simplest tasks with the colours of imagination.

Inspiration

Each Day is an opportunity for innovation. Approach your routine with the curiosity of a creator and watch as your days transform into a gallery of extraordinary moments.

Prayer

Creator of Possibilities, grant me the vision to see the artistry in my daily tasks, the courage to innovate, and the creativity to turn the ordinary into the extraordinary. Amen.

DAY 280

BALANCED WORK-LIFE INTEGRATION

Reflection

Life is a delicate dance, and finding harmony between work and personal life is an art. Reflect on the balance you seek and the rhythm you wish to establish.

Inspiration

Work and life are not opposing forces but complementary elements. In their integration, find the symphony that resonates with the melody of your extraordinary life.

Prayer

Divine Balancer, guide me in weaving a tapestry where work and life harmonise. Grant me the wisdom to prioritise, the strength to set boundaries, and the grace to enjoy both with intention. Amen.

DAY 281

ORDER IN SIMPLICITY

Reflection

Simplify your surroundings and witness the emergence of true beauty. Reflect on the elegance that simplicity brings to your life.

Inspiration

In the quiet simplicity of your space, discover the serenity that unfolds. A clutter-free environment is a canvas where the masterpiece of your life can be seen in its purest form.

Prayer

Gracious One, help me declutter my surroundings and my mind. May simplicity be the backdrop of my extraordinary life, allowing the true essence of beauty to shine through. Amen.

DAY 282

CREATIVITY UNLEASHED

Reflection

Break free from the constraints that stifle your creativity. Reflect on the boundless possibilities that unfold when you unleash your imagination. What do you see?

Inspiration

Your creativity is a force that knows no bounds. Liberate it from the shackles of doubt and routine, and watch as it transforms your world into a canvas of endless exploration.

Prayer

Muse of Creativity free my mind from creative constraints. May I embrace the vastness of my imagination and bring forth innovative expressions that colour my life with vibrancy. Amen.

DAY 283

ORGANISED INSPIRATION

Reflection

Reflect on the spaces and habits that inspire you. Create an environment that nurtures creativity, and watch as inspiration becomes a constant companion.

Inspiration

Organisation is the foundation upon which inspiration builds its home. In the orderly spaces of your life, discover the limitless possibilities that await your creative endeavours.

Prayer

Architect of Inspiration, guide me in creating spaces that breathe life into my creativity. May my surroundings be a canvas that inspires, and my habits be the brushstrokes of a beautiful life. Amen.

DAY 284

BALANCING ACTS

Reflection

Life is a series of juggling acts. Reflect on your various responsibilities and find the grace of balancing multiple roles.

Inspiration

Like a skilled performer, you can gracefully handle the different roles life presents. Embrace the challenge, and let each act be a testament to your strength and poise.

Prayer

Dear Life Force, grant me the agility to navigate the juggling acts of life with grace. May each responsibility be a step in the dance of my extraordinary life. Amen.

DAY 285

CREATIVE CUISINE

Reflection

Explore the art of nourishment through creative and balanced recipes. Reflect on the joy of preparing meals that nurture both body and soul. Pay attention to what you feed your spirit, soul and body, for we are, or will become, what we eat.

Inspiration

Specific recipes and their aromas connect with particular places and times. Food serves memory, which deepens the experience. Your kitchen is a canvas; experiment with flavours, colours, and textures, and savour the artistry of nourishing your being.

Prayer

Culinary Creator, bless my kitchen with creativity. May my meals celebrate balance, nourishment, and the joy that comes from the art of cooking. I pray my meal can unite people, mysteriously serving the emotional life. Amen.

DAY 286

STRUCTURED REFLECTION

Reflection

Reflective practices are the pillars of personal growth. Contemplate the value of structured reflection in enhancing your journey of self-discovery.

Inspiration

In the stillness of structured reflection, find the wisdom that emerges. Like a sculptor shaping clay, mould your thoughts and experiences into the masterpiece of your evolving self.

Prayer

Divine Guide, help me embrace the power of structured introspection. May my reflections mirror the beauty of my soul and the path to my extraordinary living. Amen.

DAY 287

ARTISTIC DISCIPLINE

Reflection

Reflect on the beauty of channelling creativity through disciplined artistic activities. Like a sculptor shaping marble, your commitment to artistic discipline moulds the masterpiece of your creative expression.

Inspiration

Artistic discipline is the brushstroke that gives life to your creative canvas. With each intentional act, you contribute to the gallery of your extraordinary life.

Prayer

Creative Muse, grant me the discipline to nurture and express my creativity. May my artistic actions reflect the dedication and passion I bring to the canvas of life. Amen.

DAY 288

BALANCED RELATIONSHIPS

Reflection

Relationships are the tapestry of life. Reflect on the connections that bring balance and joy, recognising the intricate threads that weave into the fabric of your existence.

Inspiration

In the dance of relationships, find the rhythm of balance. Each connection contributes to the harmony that makes your life a beautiful symphony.

Prayer

Divine Connector, guide me in cultivating relationships that bring balance and joy. May my interactions be threads of love, understanding, and shared joy in the grand tapestry of life. Amen.

DAY 289

ORGANISED FINANCES

Reflection

Reflect on the importance of taking control of your financial well-being. Like a savvy conductor orchestrating a financial symphony, reflect on the impact of structured and balanced financial practices. What comes to mind?

Inspiration

In planning your finances, find the rhythms of security and freedom. Every wise financial decision is a note that contributes to the harmonious composition of your extraordinary life.

Prayer

Source of Wealth, grant me the wisdom to manage my finances with order and balance. May my financial decisions contribute to my life's symphony of prosperity and peace.
Amen.

DAY 290

CREATIVE RESILIENCE

Reflection

Life's challenges are opportunities for creative resilience. Reflect on using creativity to bounce back, rebuild, and transform adversity into art. What can you learn?

Inspiration

Resilience is the canvas on which creativity paints its most profound strokes. In the face of challenges, let your creative spirit be the resilient artist that shapes your response to life's uncertainties.

Prayer

Eternal Refuge, infuse me with the strength to face challenges creatively. May my resilience be a work of art, demonstrating the beauty of overcoming adversity. Amen.

DAY 291

MIND-BODY HARMONY

Reflection

Explore practices that harmonise your mental and physical well-being. Reflect on the interconnected dance between mind and body, recognising the benefits of nurturing both.

Inspiration

Mind-body harmony is the choreography of a balanced life. In the synchronised movements of self-care, find the grace that allows you to dance through life with vitality and joy.

Prayer

Architect of Harmony, guide me in nurturing the delicate dance between my mind and body. May my self-care practices celebrate the beauty that arises from their harmonious partnership. Amen.

DAY 292

STRUCTURED LEARNING

Reflection

Embrace a structured approach to continuous learning and personal development. Reflect on the transformative power of knowledge and the elegance of a commitment to lifelong learning. What book/s are you currently reading?

Inspiration

Structured learning is the loom that shapes your intellectual journey. In each lesson, discover the threads that enrich the fabric of your extraordinary life.

Prayer

Custodian of Knowledge, bless me with a thirst for structured learning. May my pursuit of wisdom be guided by discipline and intention, weaving a tapestry of continuous growth. Amen.

DAY 293

INNOVATIVE SOLUTIONS

Reflection

Approach problems with creative solutions while maintaining a sense of order. Reflect on the ingenuity that arises when creativity and structure collaborate to navigate life's challenges. What comes to mind?

Inspiration

Innovation is the spark that ignites when creativity meets order. In the pursuit of solutions, let your creative mind be the compass that guides you through uncharted territories.

Prayer

Source of Innovation, grant me the creativity to see beyond challenges and the discipline to approach solutions with order. May my problem-solving be a masterpiece of inventive elegance. Amen.

DAY 294

BALANCED TECH TIME

Reflection

Find an equilibrium in using technology to enhance rather than disrupt your life. Reflect on the impact of intentional and balanced tech usage on your well-being and relationships. When was your last tech detox?

Inspiration

Technology is a tool, not a master. In the balance between screen time and real-time, discover the harmony that allows you to navigate the digital landscape while savouring the richness of the analogue world.

Prayer

Guardian of Balance, guide me in using technology to enhance my life. May I find harmony between the digital and physical realms, creating a life of balance and presence. Amen.

DAY 295

CREATIVE EXPLORATION

Reflection

Today, open the door to new creative territories. Reflect on the excitement of venturing beyond the familiar, allowing your artistic spirit to explore uncharted realms. What comes to mind?

Inspiration

Creativity flourishes in the unexplored. Embrace the thrill of creative exploration, and let the journey into the unknown expand the horizons of your artistic expression.

Prayer

Eternal All-Knowing, lead me into new creative realms. May my artistic journey be a testament to the beauty that unfolds when I venture beyond the familiar. Amen.

DAY 296

ORGANISED FITNESS

Reflection

Reflect on the importance of incorporating a well-organised fitness routine for physical and mental well-being. Consider the impact of intentional movement on your overall vitality.

Inspiration

Your body is a canvas, and fitness is the brush that sculpts strength and resilience. In the organised rhythm of your fitness routine, find the artistry of a well-nurtured body and mind.

Prayer

Dear Life Force, bless my fitness routine with order and purpose. May each movement be a strength stroke, creating a masterpiece of vitality and balance. Amen.

DAY 297

CREATIVITY IN NATURE

Reflection

Step into the embrace of nature and reflect on its beauty. Nature is a canvas of inspiration, and in its grandeur, find the muse that fuels your creative pursuits.

Inspiration

The beauty of nature is an everlasting well of inspiration. Allow the natural world's colours, sounds, and textures to infuse your creative endeavours with the richness of the earth's palette.

Prayer

Creator of Life, grant me the eyes to see the beauty around me. May the inspiration from nature flow into my creative expressions, creating a tapestry of boundless beauty.
Amen.

DAY 298

BALANCED LEISURE

Reflection

Reflect on the importance of enjoying leisure activities in moderation. Consider how balancing relaxation and productivity contributes to the richness of your life.

Inspiration

Leisure is the spice that flavours the recipe of life. In its moderation, find the perfect balance that adds depth, joy, and a touch of elegance to your daily experiences.

Prayer

Guardian of Balance, teach me the art of balanced leisure. May my moments of relaxation be a symphony of joy and my productive pursuits be a dance of purpose. Amen.

DAY 299

DESIGNED SELF-CARE

Reflection

Reflect on the significance of developing a systematic approach to self-care. Consider how intentional self-care practices contribute to your overall well-being. How can you improve on your current self-care practices?

Inspiration

Your well-being is a masterpiece, and self-care is the art that preserves its beauty. In the well-thought-out rhythm of self-care, find the balance that nurtures both body and soul.

Prayer

Lover of my Soul, guide me in developing a structured approach to self-care. May my daily self-nurturing rituals be strokes of love, creating a portrait of radiant well-being.
Amen.

DAY 300

CREATIVE COLLABORATIONS

Reflection

Today, reflect on the power of engaging in collaborative activities that spark creativity and innovation. Consider the magic that happens when creative minds come together.

Inspiration

Collaboration is the symphony of creative minds. In the dance of ideas, find the harmony that transforms individual sparks into a dazzling display of collective brilliance.

Prayer

Dear Life Force, bless my creative endeavours with a collaborative spirit. May the exchange of ideas at work and home be a melody that elevates my creative pursuits to new heights. Amen.

DAY 301

MINDFUL DAY

Reflection

On this sacred day, practice mindfulness. Centre your thoughts on the present moment, appreciating the beauty within and around you.

Inspiration

In the quietude of this day, mindfulness is the compass that guides you to the treasures of the present. Navigate the Day with awareness and discover the jewels of each moment.

Prayer

Guardian of the Present, bless me with mindful awareness today. Guide me in integrating mindfulness into my daily routine. May I savour each breath and embrace the richness of the now. Amen.

DAY 302

CREATIVE EXPRESSION IN SILENCE

Reflection

Explore the power of creative expression through moments of quiet and stillness. Reflect on the eloquence that arises when creativity speaks in the language of silence. What can you hear?

Inspiration

Silence is the canvas upon which creativity paints its most profound expressions. Discover the depth and beauty of creative expression in the quietude of stillness.

Prayer

Muse of Silence, grant me the wisdom to find creativity in the quiet moments. May my expressions in silence be a masterpiece that speaks volumes without uttering a word.
Amen.

DAY 303

OPTIMISM OVERLOAD

Reflection

Embrace the abundance of optimism. How can you view challenges as opportunities and infuse each moment with a positive perspective?

Inspiration

Optimism is the light that transforms shadows into stepping stones. Overflow with positivity and watch as your journey becomes a radiant tapestry of resilience and hope.

Prayer

Source of Hope, fill my heart with an optimism that transcends circumstances. May my outlook be a beacon of light, guiding me through challenges with grace. Amen.

DAY 304

BALANCED ENDINGS AND BEGINNINGS

Reflection

As the Day concludes, reflect on its events. Find closure in the balanced reflection of what was and prepare for the new beginning that awaits with the dawn.

Inspiration

Endings are the punctuation marks that give meaning to the sentences of our lives. Embrace the closure of the Day with gratitude, knowing that each ending is a prelude to a new and balanced beginning.

Prayer

Keeper of Time, as I reflect on the day, grant me gratitude for its lessons. May I find closure in the evening and awaken gracefully to a new dawn, ready for a balanced and creative start. Amen.

GRATITITUDE

DAY 305

THE ART OF LISTENING

Reflection

In the art of friendship, listening is the key to harmony. Reflect on how actively engaging with the thoughts and feelings of others opens the door to deeper connections and understanding.

Inspiration

Listening is an art of the heart. We find the music of genuine connection in the quiet spaces between words.

Prayer

Dear Creator, grant us the grace to listen with intention, to hear not just words but the unspoken melodies of the soul. May our friendships be a masterpiece of understanding. Amen.

DAY 306

JOYFUL CREATIVITY

Reflection

Creativity is a canvas waiting for the strokes of joy. Today, find ways to embrace the freedom to express yourself, discovering the vibrant hues of joy that creativity unveils.

Inspiration

In the dance of creativity, joy takes the lead, and every expression becomes a brushstroke on the canvas of a fulfilled heart.

Prayer

Divine Muse, infuse our creative endeavours with the brilliance of joy. May our expressions be a testament to the beauty that arises when joy and creativity intertwine. Amen.

DAY 307

LAUGHTER THERAPY

Reflection

Laughter, the universal language of joy, has the power to heal. Be intentional today; engage in the therapeutic art of laughter, allowing its infectious mirth to elevate your spirit.

Inspiration

Laughter is the chorus of a joyous heart, echoing through the corridors of our lives, dispelling shadows and inviting the sunlight of happiness.

Prayer

Healer of Hearts, bless us with the gift of laughter. May our lives be a comedy of joy, and our friendships resound with the sweet melody of shared laughter. Amen.

DAY 308

NURTURING INNER JOY

Reflection

In the sanctuary of our souls, inner joy blossoms. Reflect on ways to cultivate joy from within, independent of external circumstances.

Inspiration

Within us lies a reservoir of joy, a sacred wellspring that can quench the thirst of our spirits, regardless of the storms outside.

Prayer

Source of Eternal Joy, guide me to the well of inner happiness. May my heart be resilient, finding joy in the face of life's ebb and flow.
Amen.

DAY 309

PURSUING PASSION

Reflection

Passion is the compass guiding us to extraordinary living. Reflect on how you pursue your passions; they are the roadmaps to a life filled with purpose and fulfilment.

Inspiration

Pursuing passion, we discover the rhythm of our hearts, and every step becomes a dance towards a life well-lived.

Prayer

Creator of Passions, ignite within me the flames of purpose. May my pursuits be a testament to the extraordinary life that unfolds when passion leads the way. Amen.

DAY 310

CULTIVATING AUTHENTIC CONNECTIONS

Reflection

Authenticity is the fertile soil in the friendship garden where genuine connections take root. Reflect on the beauty that blossoms when we allow our authentic selves to flourish in the company of others.

Inspiration

Authenticity is the art of unveiling the soul, allowing friendships to bloom in the warmth of genuine connection.

Prayer

Divine Architect of Relationships, grace me with the wisdom to cultivate authentic connections. May my friendships be gardens of authenticity, where each bloom is a testament to the beauty of genuine hearts.

DAY 311

ACTS OF KINDNESS

Reflection

Kindness is the currency of true friendship, exchanged in the currency of small gestures. Reflect on the profound impact of simple acts of kindness in fortifying the bonds that tie hearts together.

Inspiration

In the ledger of friendships, every act of kindness is a priceless investment that yields dividends of joy and connection.

Prayer

Kindred Spirit, guide us to be vessels of kindness in our friendships. May my actions speak volumes of the love and warmth in my heart's depths.

DAY 312

FORGIVENESS IN FRIENDSHIPS

Reflection

Forgiveness is the elixir that rejuvenates friendships. Reflect on the liberating power of forgiveness, understanding that it is the key to nurturing lasting bonds and healing wounded hearts.

Inspiration

In the tapestry of friendships, forgiveness is the golden thread that mends even the most delicate connections.

Prayer

Healer of Hearts, grant me the strength to forgive and the humility to seek forgiveness. May my friendships be resilient, adorned with the grace of second chances.

DAY 313

CELEBRATING DIFFERENCES

Reflection

Diversity is the kaleidoscope that enriches the canvas of friendship. Reflect on the vibrant beauty that emerges when we celebrate and embrace the differences that make each friend a unique masterpiece.

Inspiration

In the mosaic of friendships, each unique piece contributes to the masterpiece of collective harmony.

Prayer

Artisan of Unity, help me appreciate the beauty in diversity. May my friendships be a testament to the richness that arises when differences are celebrated and honoured.

DAY 314

QUALITY VS. QUANTITY

Reflection

In the grand ballroom of friendships, quality outshines quantity. Reflect on the value of deep, meaningful connections over a superficial multitude, understanding that a few trustworthy friends can illuminate the darkest nights.

Inspiration

In the constellation of friendships, the bright stars of quality guide us through life's vastness.

Prayer

Connector of Hearts, lead me to discernment in my friendships. May my circle be small but brilliant, filled with the warmth of quality connections.

DAY 315

LOYALTY AND TRUST

Reflection

Trust is the foundation, and loyalty is the fortress of true friendships. Reflect on the importance of building a sanctuary of trust and loyalty, where hearts find security and camaraderie.

Inspiration

Trust is the cornerstone of the citadel of friendships, and loyalty is the noble guardian standing strong against the winds of doubt.

Prayer

Keeper of Trust, guide me to be trustworthy and loyal in my friendships. May our bonds be unshakable, built on the pillars of integrity and commitment. Amen.

DAY 316

NURTURING FRIENDSHIPS IN BUSY LIVES

Reflection

In the bustling ballroom of life, friendships can quickly be overshadowed by the dance of busy schedules. Reflect on the importance of intentional effort and thoughtful gestures to maintain strong connections amidst the chaos of daily life.

Inspiration

Like rare jewels, friendships require care and attention. In the busy rhythm of life, let us be virtuoso dancers, gracefully weaving our friends into the symphony of our days.

Prayer

Creator of Time, grant me the wisdom to prioritise and nurture my friendships amid the demands of life's dance. May our bonds grow more robust, even amid life's grand performance. Amen.

DAY 317

FINDING JOY IN SIMPLE PLEASURES

Reflection

Amidst the grand tapestry of life, joy often hides in the folds of simplicity. Reflect on the art of finding joy in the every day, appreciating the subtle beauty that weaves through the fabric of our existence.

Inspiration

In the quiet moments and simple pleasures, joy unfurls its wings. It is in the most minor notes that life's sweetest melodies are often found.

Prayer

Dear Life Force, teach me to dance to the rhythm of simplicity. May our hearts be attuned to the gentle cadence of life's simple pleasures, and may joy be our constant companion. Amen.

DAY 318

GRATITUDE FOR JOY

Reflection

Gratitude is the golden key that unlocks the door to a joy-filled heart. Reflect on the transformative power of gratitude in amplifying the joy that we experience in our daily lives.

Inspiration

Gratitude is the prism through which joy refracts into a spectrum of blessings. In counting our joys, we multiply them.

Prayer

Architect of Blessings, help me to build a foundation of gratitude in my heart. May our days be filled with the echoes of 'thank you,' and may joy multiply as we recognise and appreciate life's gifts. Amen.

DAY 319

EMBRACING LAUGHTER

Reflection

Laughter is the music that transcends language and lifts the spirit. Reflect on the therapeutic power of laughter, understanding its ability to lighten the heaviest of hearts.

Inspiration

In the grand orchestration of life, laughter is the sweetest melody. Its notes, like bubbles, rise to the surface, carrying away the weight of the mundane.

Prayer

Lover of my Soul, grant me the gift of mirth. May our lives be a symphony of joy, and may the laughter we share with others be the chorus that echoes through the corridors of our days. Amen.

DAY 320

JOY IN GIVING

Reflection

In the act of giving, joy finds its most profound expression. Reflect on the transformative power of helping and giving to others, understanding that true joy is often discovered in the service of others.

Inspiration

The dance of joy is never more elegant than when it twirls in the grace of giving. In our generosity, we find the true richness of the soul.

Prayer

Giver of Grace, guide us to be generous spirits. May our hands be open, our hearts be giving, and may the joy of our generosity radiate to those around us. Amen.

DAY 321

MINDFULNESS AND JOY

Reflection

In the present moment, joy finds its truest form. Reflect on mindfulness practice, understanding how being fully present enhances the richness of our joy-filled experiences.

Inspiration

Mindfulness is the art of savouring each moment's flavour; joy becomes the sweetest nectar in this attentive tasting.

Prayer

Master of Moments, anchor us in the present. May our minds be vessels of mindfulness, and may joy flow into our lives as we drink deeply from the cup of each passing moment. Amen.

DAY 322

CULTIVATING A POSITIVE MINDSET

Reflection

The mind is a garden, and positivity is the sunlight that makes it flourish. Reflect on the power of cultivating a positive mindset, understanding that the seeds of joy bloom in the fertile soil of optimistic thinking.

Inspiration

Positivity is the gentle rain that nourishes the garden of the mind. In its embrace, joy blossoms in vibrant hues.

Prayer

Divine Spirit of Positivity, help me to tend to the garden of my mind. May my thoughts be seeds of optimism, and may the flowers of joy bloom abundantly in the sunlight of positivity. Amen.

DAY 323

JOYFUL RELATIONSHIPS

Reflection

In the dance of life, relationships are the graceful waltz that elevates our existence. Reflect on the profound impact of positive relationships, understanding that they are the pillars supporting the architecture of a joyful life.

Inspiration

Relationships are the threads weaving the tapestry of joy. In embracing positive connections, life's symphony becomes a melody of happiness.

Prayer

Eternal Connector, grace our lives with the elegance of positive connections. May our relationships be sources of joy, each interaction a step in the graceful dance towards a life adorned with happiness. Amen.

DAY 324

HAPPINESS IN GIVING

Reflection

In the art of giving, happiness finds its most radiant expression. Reflect on the joy that emanates from acts of generosity, understanding that giving is also a gift to the giver. In what way can you expand your giving?

Inspiration

Giving is the alchemy of joy. In the offering of self, we discover the golden elixir that transforms the mundane into the extraordinary.

Prayer

Bestower of Blessings, guide our hands in acts of giving. May the joy of generosity flow through us, enriching our lives and the lives of those who receive our gifts. Amen.

DAY 325

FRIENDSHIPS THAT INSPIRE HAPPINESS

Reflection

Happiness blossoms like a rare and exquisite flower in the sanctuary of friendship. Reflect on the pivotal role of supportive friendships in nurturing your joy. What can you learn?

Inspiration

Friendships are the gardens of happiness, where each bloom is watered by the shared joys and sorrows of kindred spirits.

Prayer

Connector of Souls, bless me with the grace of a supportive community. May my friendships inspire and cultivate happiness, and may I, in turn, be a source of joy for my friends. Amen.

DAY 326

THE RIPPLE EFFECT OF HAPPINESS

Reflection

Like a stone dropped into a pond, happiness creates ripples that extend far beyond the point of impact. Reflect on the profound truth that your happiness has the power to positively influence your broader community.

Inspiration

The ripple of individual happiness becomes the gentle wave that bathes the shores of the collective, transforming communities into havens of joy.

Prayer

Source of Radiant Joy, may our happiness send positivity into the world. May our joy be a catalyst for uplifting the spirits of those around us. Amen.

DAY 327

THE PURSUIT OF AUTHENTIC HAPPINESS

Reflection

In the labyrinth of life, the pursuit of happiness is a quest for authenticity. Reflect on the common misconceptions about happiness and challenge yourself to seek the genuine, enduring joy that resides within.

Inspiration

Pursuing authentic happiness is not a race but a journey of self-discovery. In knowing oneself, we unlock the treasure chest of enduring joy.

Prayer

Divine Guide, lead me in the pursuit of genuine happiness. May my quest be marked by self-awareness and authenticity, and may the joy I discover be profound and lasting. Amen.

DAY 328

CREATING A HAPPY ENVIRONMENT

Reflection

Our surroundings are the canvas upon which the masterpiece of our lives is painted. Reflect on the importance of crafting a happy environment, understanding that your external surroundings influence your internal landscape.

Inspiration

The spaces we inhabit are the stages upon which the drama of our lives unfolds. In creating a happy environment, we become the architects of our joy.

Prayer

Designer of the Universe, inspire me to craft environments that reflect my inner happiness. May my home and workplace be sanctuaries of joy, fostering an atmosphere of positivity and well-being. Amen.

DAY 329

BALANCING WORK AND HAPPINESS

Reflection

Finding balance is the key to sustaining happiness in the delicate dance between work and life. Reflect on the equilibrium between your career pursuits and personal well-being and ways to infuse true happiness, one that emerges from a harmonious blend of both.

Inspiration

Balance is the art of juggling work responsebilities and life's pleasures. In the delicate dance, we find the rhythm that sustains happiness.

Prayer

Harmony-Maker, guide me in the dance of balance. May my pursuits be fruitful, and may my life be a testament to the exquisite harmony that arises when work and happiness waltz together. Amen.

DAY 330

OVERCOMING CHALLENGES WITH HAPPINESS

Reflection

In the theatre of life, challenges often take centre stage. Reflect on the resilience that blooms within you when happiness becomes a guiding light through the storm, empowering you to face adversity with grace.

Inspiration

Like a flower that thrives in the harshest soil, happiness becomes the anchor that helps us weather life's storms with unwavering strength.

Prayer

Divine Light, grant me the strength to find happiness even in the shadow of challenges. May my spirit be resilient, and may the glow of joy guide me through the darkest hours.
Amen.

DAY 331

THE ROLE OF SELF-LOVE IN HAPPINESS

Reflection

Self-love is the nourishing soil from which joy blossoms in the garden of happiness. Reflect on the benefits of cultivating a deep well of love and care for yourself as the foundation for sustained happiness.

Inspiration

Self-love is the gentle rain that bathes the seeds of happiness within us. In its embrace, our hearts bloom with the radiant flowers of joy.

Prayer

Nurturer of Souls, grant me the grace to tend to the garden of self-love. May my reflections be a gentle mirror and embrace myself with the same tenderness I offer to cherished friends. Amen.

DAY 332

LETTING GO FOR HAPPINESS

Reflection

In the elegant dance of life, letting go is the graceful turn that leads to happiness. Reflect on the power of releasing negativity and embracing the freedom of a lighter heart.

Inspiration

Letting go is the art of releasing the balloons of negativity, allowing our spirits to soar into the boundless sky of happiness.

Prayer

Liberator of Souls, grant me the courage to let go of what weighs me down. May my heart be unburdened, and may the winds of joy carry me to new heights. Amen.

DAY 333

REFLECTING ON RELATIONSHIP GROWTH

Reflection

Take a moment to reflect on the journey of your relationship. Consider the growth you've experienced individually and together. How have challenges shaped you, and what strengths have emerged from shared trials? Acknowledge the beauty in the evolution of your connection.

Inspiration

Relationships are like gardens—nurtured, they bloom with vibrant life. Today, reflect on the growth you've cultivated together. In every challenge, find the seeds of strength; in every triumph, see the blossoms of love. Embrace the beauty of your journey.

Prayer

Eternal love, bless our relationship with the grace of growth. May the challenges we face become fertile ground for resilience, and may the joys we celebrate be the blossoms of our shared journey. Guide us as we continue to cultivate a love that flourishes. Amen.

DAY 334

HAPPINESS IN SHARED MOMENTS

Reflection

In the treasury of memories, shared moments with friends are the jewels that gleam with happiness. Reflect on the beauty of these moments, understanding that they are the gems that enrich the fabric of your life.

Inspiration

Shared moments with friends are the bookmarks in the story of our lives. In their presence, happiness becomes the golden thread that stitches our stories together.

Prayer

Keeper of Memories, thank you for the gift of shared moments. May our hearts be filled with gratitude, and may the happiness we experience with friends become the golden chapters in the book of our lives. Amen.

DAY 335

BLOSSOMING DREAMS

Reflection

As the year begins to roll its carpet, take a moment to identify the dreams within you, ready to blossom. Like delicate flowers, they await your care and attention.

Inspiration

Your dreams are seeds waiting for the right moment to bloom. Nurture them with belief, water them with persistence, and watch the beauty unfold."

Prayer

Dear God, I plant the seeds of possibility in the garden of my aspirations. I pray my dreams grow with grace, and may I tend to them with style and dedication. Amen.

DAY 336

SEEDS OF INTENTION

Reflection

Today, let's sow the seeds of intention. What goals do you wish to achieve this month? What actions can you take to ensure they flourish?

Inspiration

Intentions are the roots of our desires. Plant them with purpose, water them with dedication, and witness the abundant harvest they bring.

Prayer

Creator of Life, I plant the seeds of purpose in the fertile soil of my intentions. I pray my actions to be the sunlight that nurtures them into a fruitful reality. Amen.

DAY 337

WINTER'S FERTILE GROUND

Reflection

Even in the winter of life, opportunities lay hidden beneath the snow. What opportunities can you uncover in the stillness of this season?

Inspiration

Winter is a silent gardener, preparing the ground for the vibrant life to come. Seek the hidden opportunities and let them bloom in their own time."

Prayer

Eternal Presence, in the quiet of winter's embrace, I discover the hidden treasures of opportunity. May I patiently await the right season for their blossoming. Amen.

DAY 338

GRATEFUL HEARTS

Reflection

Gratitude is the fertilizer for a bountiful life. Reflect on the abundance that surrounds you, nurturing your grateful hearts.

Inspiration

In gratitude, I find the true richness of life. Cherish the big and small blessings that paint the canvas of our existence.

Prayer

Dear God, with a heart full of gratitude, I embrace life's abundance. May I appreciate each moment with style and thanksgiving. Amen.

DAY 339

THE GIFT OF PRESENCE

Reflection

In the hustle of life, the present moment is a jewel waiting to be discovered. Today, treasure the gift of being present.

Inspiration

Presence is the key that unlocks the door to joy. Find fortune in the beauty of now, for it is a precious gift that enriches our lives.

Prayer

Eternal Presence, in the tapestry of time, I weave the threads of Presence. I pray to cherish each moment, finding fortune in the beauty of now. Amen.

DAY 340

KALEIDOSCOPE OF BLESSINGS

Reflection

Life unfolds in a myriad of blessings. Take time toDay to appreciate the diverse forms of good fortune that colour your world.

Inspiration

Blessings come in many shapes and sizes, each a unique colour in the kaleidoscope of life. Embrace the diversity, for it is the true wealth of existence.

Prayer

Gracious God, with gratitude in my heart, I acknowledge the kaleidoscope of blessings that enrich my life. May I be open to the diversity of fortune that unfolds each day.
Amen.

DAY 341

JOYFUL TRADITIONS

Reflection

In the tapestry of our lives, traditions are the threads that weave joy into our story. What traditions bring you joy, and how can you create new ones this season?

Inspiration

Traditions are the timeless melodies that resonate in our hearts. Celebrate them with style, creating harmonies that echo through generations.

Prayer

Eternal Joy, in the dance of time, I celebrate the joyous traditions that connect me to the past and create a legacy for the future. I pray each tradition to be a note in the symphony of my extraordinary living. Amen.

DAY 342

LAUGHTER'S SYMPHONY

Reflection

Laughter is the music of the soul, a symphony that resonates with joy. How can you infuse more laughter into your life and share this melody with others?

Inspiration

Laughter is the sweetest melody, a universal language that brings hearts together. Tune into the joyous symphony of laughter and let it be your soundtrack."

Prayer

Dear Life Force, I dance to the laughter's symphony in the grand ballroom of life. May my heart be light, and may the music of joy echo through every corner of my existence. Amen.

DAY 343

DANCE OF CELEBRATION

Reflection

Life is a dance, and each moment is a step in the choreography of your journey. How can you infuse your steps with gratitude and merriment today?

Inspiration

Celebrate the dance of life, twirling through each moment with grace and gratitude. Every step is a celebration, every breath a note in the melody of existence.

Prayer

Benevolent God, with gratitude in my heart, I join the dance of celebration. May my every step be a stylish expression of joy, and may my spirit twirl with the rhythm of gratitude. Amen.

DAY 344

MAGIC WITHIN

Reflection

Within us lies a magic, an enchantment waiting to be discovered. What sparks of magic can you find within yourself today, leading to extraordinary living?

Inspiration

The magic within is the key to an extraordinary life. Look within, discover your enchantment, and let it illuminate the path to joy and fulfilment.

Prayer

Divine Presence, in the quiet sanctuary of my soul, I uncover the magic within. May this enchantment guide me to a life of style, grace, and extraordinary living. Amen.

DAY 345

SOULFUL ILLUMINATION

Reflection

Today, let's focus on nurturing the inner light that guides us. How can you illuminate your soul and radiate that light into the world around you?

Inspiration

Within every soul, there is a radiant light waiting to shine. Nurture that light, let it illuminate your path, and may it be a beacon for others.

Prayer

Lover of my Soul, I tend to the flame of illumination in the divine ballroom of my soul. I pray my inner light shines brightly, casting a stylish glow on my life journey.
Amen.

DAY 346

EMBRACING CHANGE

Reflection

Change is the fertile ground where new beginnings take root. What changes in your life can you embrace today, recognising the growth potential?

Inspiration

Embrace change as a gardener embraces spring. Discover the seeds of new possibilities and the blooms of a renewed spirit in the fertile ground of transformation.

Prayer

Divine Grace, with Grace in my heart, I embrace the changing seasons of life. May each transition be stylish, bringing forth the blossoms of extraordinary living. Amen.

DAY 347

SEASON OF MIRACLES

Reflection

The season of miracles surrounds us. What miracles, both big and small, can you trust in and invite into your life today?

Inspiration

Miracles are the whispers of magic in our lives. Trust in the season's enchantment and open your heart to the extraordinary possibilities that await.

Prayer

Miracle Maker, in the sacred dance of life, I open my heart to the season of miracles. May each Day be adorned with the magic that leads to extraordinary living. Amen.

DAY 348

ALIGNING WITH ABUNDANCE

Reflection

As we enter a new season, let's align our thoughts and actions with the abundance surrounding us. How can we attract good fortune through positive alignment?

Inspiration

Align your thoughts with the frequency of abundance. In the dance of life, positive vibrations attract the prosperity that awaits. Tune into the frequency of success.

Prayer

Abundant life, in the symphony of life, I align my spirit with the melodies of abundance. May positive vibrations resonate within me, attracting the good fortune that graces my path. Amen.

DAY 349

WAVES OF PROSPERITY

Reflection
Today, you can visualise the ebb and flow of prosperity in every aspect of life. What areas can you envision being touched by the waves of abundance?

Inspiration
Prosperity is a rhythm that dances through every corner of our existence. Visualise the waves of abundance flowing effortlessly, touching and enriching every aspect of your life.

Prayer
Giver of Wealth, as the tides of prosperity roll in, I visualise the waves touching every realm of my being. May the flow of abundance be graceful and harmonious, bringing prosperity in every wave. Amen.

DAY 350

GOLDEN OPPORTUNITIES

Reflection

Seize the golden moments that lead to prosperity. What opportunities are shimmering around you today, waiting to be embraced?

Inspiration

Opportunities, like golden sunbeams, illuminate our path to prosperity. Seize them with grace and enthusiasm, for in their glow lies the promise of a prosperous journey.

Prayer

Opportunities Giver, in the theatre of life, I take centre stage and seize the golden opportunities that await. May my steps be stylish, and may each opportunity lead to a prosperous act in the play of my life. Amen.

DAY 351

MERRY HEARTS

Reflection

Infuse each Day with the merry spirit of the season. How can you bring joy and merriment into your heart and the hearts of those around you?

Inspiration

A merry heart is a timeless accessory that never goes out of style. Let the spirit of joy be your daily fashion, and wear it with grace and flair.

Prayer

Lover of my Soul, with a heart adorned in merriment, I step into the day's grand ballroom. May my spirit dance with joy, and may the melody of merriment echo through every moment. Amen.

DAY 352

JOYFUL GENEROSITY

Reflection

Today, find joy in giving and sharing with others. How can you generously present to someone, offering your time, attention, or kindness?

Inspiration

Generosity is the couture of the soul. Find joy in giving, for in the act of generosity, both the giver and the receiver are adorned with the elegance of compassion.

Prayer

Destiny Designer, in the wardrobe of my spirit, I choose the attire of generosity. May my actions be a stylish expression of kindness, and may joy be the accessory that completes the ensemble. Amen.

DAY 353

SEASONAL SERENITY

Reflection

Create a serene space for merriment and joy. How can you cultivate a peaceful environment that allows the merry spirit of the season to flourish?

Inspiration

Serenity is the canvas upon which the colours of joy and merriment paint their masterpiece. Create a tranquil space and let the season's spirit dance peacefully.

Prayer

Eternal Peace, in the sanctuary of serenity, I find Peace and joy. May my surroundings be adorned with tranquillity, creating a canvas for the merry spirit of the season to unfold.
Amen.

DAY 354

MINDFUL LIVING

Reflection

In the hustle of the season, let's pause to cultivate mindfulness. What aspects of your life can benefit from mindful attention today?

Inspiration

Mindful living is the art of savouring each moment. In the stillness of awareness, we find the harmony that elevates ordinary moments into extraordinary experiences.

Prayer

Eternal Peace, I embrace the present moment in the elegance of mindfulness. May my actions be graceful, and may the beauty of each moment be a testament to the art of mindful living. Amen.

DAY 355

SACRED SPACES

Reflection

Today, reflect on the spaces you occupy. How can you create environments that inspire fertility, fortune, and joy?

Inspiration

Our surroundings reflect our inner world. Design sacred spaces that mirror the abundance you wish to attract, cultivating an atmosphere of inspiration and positivity.

Prayer

Sacred One, in the sanctuary of my spaces, I invoke the spirit of fertility, fortune, and joy. May each corner be adorned with grace, and may my surroundings inspire a life of extraordinary living. Amen.

DAY 356

DIVINE ALIGNMENT

Reflection

Today, connect with the divine forces that guide your journey. How can you align your actions with the higher purpose that brings meaning and fulfilment to your life?

Inspiration

Divine alignment is the compass that leads us to our true north. In the symphony of existence, attune your spirit to the harmonies of purpose and guidance.

Prayer

Dear God, with reverence in my heart, I seek divine alignment. May my journey be guided by the forces of grace, and may each step be in harmony with the divine plan. Amen.

DAY 357

SERENADE OF THE SPIRIT

Reflection

Today, reflect on the spiritual melodies that bring harmony. What practices or moments elevate your spirit and give your soul a sense of serenade?

Inspiration

The spirit dances to the melody of the soul. In the quiet moments of serenade, find the tunes that bring peace, joy, and harmony to your inner world.

Prayer

Divine Spirit, in the ballroom of my spirit, I listen to the serenade that echoes through my soul. May the harmonies of peace and joy soundtrack my inner journey. Amen.

DAY 358

BALANCING ACT

Reflection
Life is a balancing act. Where can you bring equilibrium to the various aspects of your life for holistic well-being?

Inspiration
Balance is the art of harmonising the diverse elements of life. In the dance of responsebilities and passions, find the rhythm that nurtures your well-being.

Prayer
Source of Life, in the choreography of life, I strive for balance. May my steps be graceful, my movements intentional, and may the dance of my life be a harmonious masterpiece. Amen.

DAY 359

DIVINE FESTIVITIES

Reflection

Celebrate the divine within and around you. How can you infuse the season's festivities with reverence and spiritual grace?

Inspiration

Every celebration is a sacred dance with the divine. Infuse your festivities with gratitude, joy, and acknowledgement of the divine presence in every moment.

Prayer

Gracious God, I recognise the divine within and around me in the grand celebration of life. May my festivities be adorned with gratitude, and may joy be the crown of each sacred moment. Amen.

DAY 360

FESTIVE GRATITUDE

Reflection

As we immerse ourselves in the festive season, take a moment to express gratitude. What brings you joy during this time, and how can you appreciate the richness of these moments?

Inspiration

In the dance of festivities, gratitude is the rhythm that elevates the joy. Thanks for the magic surrounding you, and let gratitude adorn your days like a stylish accessory.

Prayer

Dear God, I adorn my heart with the jewels of gratitude in the grand ballroom of gratitude. May each festive moment be a testament to the elegance of appreciation. Amen.

DAY 361

ETERNAL JOY

Reflection

Today, embrace the everlasting joy that comes from within. Reflect on the inner sources of pleasure that transcend external circumstances. What inner joys can you tap into that transcend the transient nature of external circumstances?

Inspiration

True joy is a timeless treasure, a melody that plays from the depths of our soul. Embrace the everlasting joy within, for it is a symphony that resonates through all seasons.

Prayer

Gracious God, in the sanctuary of my soul, I discover the eternal spring of joy. May my heart dance to the rhythm of inner happiness, a stylish expression that transcends the passing of time. Amen.

DAY 362

REFLECTIONS OF THE YEAR

Reflection

Today, reflect on the growth and blessings of the past year. What milestones and lessons have shaped your journey, and how have they graced your path?

Inspiration

Reflection is the mirror that reveals the beauty of our journey. Each reflection is a stroke on the canvas of our lives, creating a masterpiece of growth and blessings.

Prayer

Faithful God, in the gallery of reflections, I acknowledge the artistry of my past year. May the colours of growth and blessings create a masterpiece that inspires my future steps. Amen.

DAY 363

REFLECTIVE RESILIENCE

Reflection

Grow stronger through reflections on the year. How have challenges and setbacks contributed to your resilience and strength?

Inspiration

Resilience is the art of turning setbacks into comebacks. Reflect on the challenges faced with a heart full of courage, for they have sculpted your resilient spirit.

Prayer

Courageous God, with reflective resilience, I embrace the past year's challenges. May the scars be marks of strength, and may I walk forward with grace and unwavering courage. Amen.

DAY 364

NEW YEAR'S MAGIC

Reflection

As the year draws close, welcome the magic of new beginnings with open hearts. What fresh possibilities and opportunities await in the coming year?

Inspiration

The magic of new beginnings is the spark that ignites the flames of hope. Approach the coming year with open hearts, for within it lies the potential for extraordinary possibilities.

Prayer

Miraculous One, in the enchanting realm of new beginnings, I open my heart to the magic of the coming year. May the possibilities be endless and my journey be filled with grace and style. Amen.

DAY 365

FERTILE RESOLUTIONS

Reflection

Today, set intentions for a fertile and prosperous New Year. What resolutions can you plant as seeds for growth and abundance in the days ahead?

Inspiration

Resolutions are the fertile soil in which our aspirations take root. Choose resolutions that nourish the garden of your dreams, cultivating a landscape of prosperity.

Prayer

Gracious God, I plant the seeds of fertile resolutions in the garden of possibilities. May my intentions blossom into a landscape of prosperity, and may the coming year be abundant in grace. Amen.

WITH THANKS AND APPRECIATION

There is a saying that it takes a village to raise a child; it takes a similarly connected community to create a book, and I'm grateful to all the marvellous people who helped me put this book together. For sure, the words are all mine. The layout design that makes Extraordinary Living easy to read is my creativity.

To the fantastic ladies in my "His Lady" group, your camaraderie has been a lighthouse, guiding this literary voyage - thank you for the honour.

To Alexandra, Feyi, Lamide, Mena, and Wese, for the blessings of friendship and constant back-and-forths. I cannot thank you enough.

My son, Alex, your boundless love and inspiration have painted these pages with hues of warmth and joy.

To you, my dear reader, who now carry the essence of this book into your extraordinary life. Your journey will be adorned with the fragrance of grace, and may each page be a stepping stone towards a life of extraordinary living.

I only pray that all who helped me bring this extraordinary book into complete being can read my affection, appreciation, and gratitude between every line.

Boundless blessings to you.

ALSO BY AJI R. MICHAEL

OPEN TO LOVE: A Modern Woman's Memoir on Being Single and Happy

HIS LADY: 5 Traits of a Godly Ambitious Woman

THE PURPOSE-DRIVEN CAREER: 3 Breakthrough Steps to Fnd Happiness; Joy, and Fulfilment in Your Career

AUTHOR

Aji R. Michael is a master coach, life stylist, and bestselling author of several books centred around personal transformation. Through her books, podcasts, videos and other resources, Aji has helped many professionals become healthy, elegant and fulfilled.

Over a decade of experience in the fast-paced health and care sector led her to founding Redefining Living. A social enterprise dedicated to empowering today's workforce by providing tools, education and digital resources to create their own version of everyday brilliance.

www.ingramcontent.com/pod-product-compliance
Lightning Source LLC
Chambersburg PA
CBHW070050230426
43661CB00005B/839